Francis Tilney Bassett

**The Book of the Prophet Hosea**

Francis Tilney Bassett

**The Book of the Prophet Hosea**

ISBN/EAN: 9783743414662

Manufactured in Europe, USA, Canada, Australia, Japa

Cover: Foto ©Lupo / pixelio.de

Manufactured and distributed by brebook publishing software (www.brebook.com)

Francis Tilney Bassett

**The Book of the Prophet Hosea**

THE

# Book of the Prophet Hosea,

LITERALLY TRANSLATED,

WITH INTRODUCTION

AND

NOTES CRITICAL AND EXPLANATORY.

BY THE

REV. F. TILNEY BASSETT, M.A.,

SOMETIME SCHOLAR OF GONVILLE AND CAIUS COLLEGE, CAMBRIDGE, AND
SUNDAY MORNING LECTURER OF OLD WIDCOMBE CHURCH, BATH.

LONDON: W. MACINTOSH, 24, PATERNOSTER ROW.
BATH: R. C. PEACH, 8, BRIDGE STREET.

1869.

# PREFACE.

In giving publicity to the following translation of the Prophet Hosea, it may be well to state that the precise object the writer has in view, is to convey to the English reader the native cast and character which these prophecies present in their Hebrew protoplast; and thus to furnish, as nearly as possible, in our own tongue a facsimile of the original. To attain this end—

1. The most exact and literal rendering of the Hebrew text has been adhered to, and in a few places only has the necessity of the case introduced an exception to this rule.

2. The same word in English has been employed to reproduce the same word in the original, with the exception of some prepositions and conjunctions, and in a few other instances, where the idioms of the two languages, or other special reasons, have rendered a slight variation necessary.

3. The position of the words in the original has been preserved, it is hoped without incurring the charge of obscurity. In most versions this order of the Hebrew arrangement has been almost wantonly disregarded, so that not only has the nervous expression of thought, and the point of a striking

antithesis, been frequently weakened and lost, but the proper emphasis also, so necessary to the intelligent comprehension of Holy Scripture, been rendered uncertain, and sometimes even transferred to the wrong word. This rule also, it may be added, has been violated on but a few occasions.

4. In arranging the parallelisms and the punctuation generally, the accents which from time immemorial have been affixed to the Hebrew text, have been followed as a guide. It is to be regretted that our own punctuation supplies so few facilities for representing the complex but perfect system of Hebrew accentuation. At the utmost we can only reproduce, and even that but imperfectly, the larger and more important members of this body-guard of the sacred text, which have been compared to emperors, kings, and lords in the dominion of Hebrew literature, but those that are more feeble, but perhaps not less necessary for the exact disposition and arrangement of words in a sentence, must be lost to us, or only supplied in thought. We may listen to the word of command uttered by the leaders to their battalions, but the directions of the subalterns and sergeants to their respective companies and quaternions fail to reach our ear; to say nothing of the conjunctive accents, whose office is not to separate or disjoin, but to link and group together words in a clause—" stops to tell you to go on," as they have been facetiously defined. These minute companions of the text have

been duly consulted, and the hints they convey not been disregarded.

Those who have studied the translations of our prophet, ancient and modern, English and Continental, will see how far the present effort has been aided by those which have gone before, and how far a servile following of authorities has been avoided. Some critics have proposed emendations of the text where the language appears to be difficult or hopelessly obscure; these are really only so many confessions of ignorance of the meaning of the prophet, as he has been handed down to us, or exhibitions of their own ingenuity. Such liberties with God's Holy Word I emphatically repudiate. Scripture is not an enigma for theologians or critics to sit round like a party of children at a puzzle or a labyrinth, to guess at solutions or to escape by force or fraud from difficulties. Our duty is not to distort the text which Providence has preserved to us, to make it square with theories that have their birth in individual minds, and which therefore can have no weight with others who are qualified to think for themselves, or to pass off private hypotheses as ascertained truth, to impose upon the multitude, but to translate the text fairly, as it stands, and where we cannot unravel the tangled skein by the proper laws of language, to confess the difficulty, and not rudely to pull the ark to pieces and patch it up again with man's devices, in a vain endeavour to disclose and explain its mysteries. At the same time, when MSS.

vary, when ancient versions, such as the Septuagint, Syriac, and Latin Vulgate, or the relics of Aquila, Symmachus, and Theodotion, &c., are unanimous in their testimony, or a majority of them point to a particular reading, such evidence should command, to say the least, the respect and consideration of every translator.

In the notes brevity has been studied. In all difficult and disputed passages the renderings of the versions above mentioned, together with those of the Targum, have been appended to the note, by which it will generally appear—a matter of consolation if not of information to ourselves—that the texts which present difficulties to us now wore the same features in days of old, and as doctors disagree now, so they did then; but the long lists of modern authorities, so common in works of this kind, have been purposely omitted, except when strictly necessary. Their assistance has, it is needless to say, been fully felt and appreciated, but there is neither pleasure nor profit to the ordinary reader to find every page encumbered with an ever-recurring pedigree of critics. It is sufficient to say that they have been for the most part consulted, their opinions severally weighed, compared, accepted, or discarded.

It may be well, for the sake of the general reader, to take a brief glance at the origin and history of the ancient versions and authorities referred to in the notes. The first and most important is, beyond all question, the version of the Septuagint. Various are the accounts given of the first formation of this translation. Tradition and fable have been busy in spinning their cobwebs, to conceal the early history of this effort to clothe the Word of God in a foreign garb. Some points, however, are clear and incontrovertible; that it was commenced in the early part of the second century B.C., (about 280;) that it was the work of Jews, and that the task was performed at Alexandria, and probably at the request of Ptolemy, the king of Egypt; that it received its name either from being the work of seventy-two interpreters, as an old writer on the subject tells us, or because it was approved of by the Sanhedrin. This version was received by the Jews with great favour, and was of general use with "the dispersed among the Gentiles," from whom it passed to the early Christian Church, and was received by them as the "authorized version of the Old Testament Scriptures."

During the second century of the Christian era other Greek versions of the Old Testament were made. Aquila, who was a Jew, or a proselyte to Judaism, undertook the task of translation, chiefly with a view to assist the Jews in their controversy with Christians, who pressed them closely with arguments derived from the Septuagint version. That translation, as we have seen, had been held by the Jews in the highest veneration till the Church employed its testimony polemically against the synagogue, when their love turned to hatred, and the Jews who, according to Philo, had kept a yearly festival in honour of its completion, now proclaimed a fast on the eighth of Thebet, for the purpose of execrating the day on which it was made. Aquila's translation was promoted to the throne from which the Septuagint had been deposed, and its renderings being slavishly exact and literal, so much so, as frequently to be in open violation of the idioms of the Greek language, was entitled " the Hebrew verity," and was read publicly in their synagogues.

Theodotion also executed a translation of the Old Testament, or as some think, revised the Septuagint version with the Hebrew text. According to the testimony of Eusebius and Jerome, he was a member of the sect of the Ebionites Both Aquila and Theodotion are accused by Irenæus of corrupting Messianic passages.

Symmachus also put forth a translation of the Hebrew Scriptures in the Greek language. Little is known of him, except that Eusebius states that he was an Ebionite, and Epiphanius tells us that he was first a Samaritan, then a Jew, next a Christian, and last of all an Ebionite. His translation was not so close as that of Aquila, but rather aimed at an elegant style.

There were also three other versions discovered by Origen, known as the fifth, sixth, and seventh versions. Of these, fragments only of the fifth, marked E, have come down to us of our Prophet.

Of all these translations (except the Septuagint)

only portions have been preserved to us amongst the relics of Origen's Hexapla.

Besides these Greek versions, the Latin Vulgate was made by Jerome, direct from the Hebrew text, (except the Psalms, which were derived, through the old Italic version, from the Septuagint,) at the close of the fourth century. This translation has passed through many revisions and editions, but still remains a valuable witness of the text of Holy Writ.

The Syriac version is also a testimony of great importance; for although we may not give credence to the traditions concerning it—that portions of the Old Testament were translated in Solomon's time, at the request of Hiram, king of Tyre, or that translators were sent from Palestine by the Apostle Thaddeus, or by Abgarus, king of Edessa—yet it is only right to infer that its origin is lost in the dim distance of antiquity. The Old Testament was rendered direct from the Hebrew original, according to the testimony of Bar-Hebræus, which is confirmed by internal evidence. It is a literal and faithful translation, and perhaps the most reliable of all the ancient versions.

The Targum which contains the minor prophets, known as the Targum of Jonathan ben-Uzziel, is very generally now-a-days ascribed to Joseph the Blind, who flourished in the fourth century. The work forms a running commentary on the sacred text. The rise of this system of interpretation is thought to have commenced in the time of Ezra, at the return from Babylon, when the people had become unfamiliarised with their mother tongue. It is an interesting study to examine the explanations contained in this commentary, as in many places, beyond doubt, very ancient traditional interpretations have been preserved to us.

For these authorities use has been made of Tischendorf's edition of the Septuagint; for the other Greek versions, Montfaucon's Origen's Hexapla, (it is to be regretted that the valuable edition of Field, now in course of publication, has not yet reached our prophet;) for the Vulgate, the Paris edition of 1852; and for the Syriac and Targum, the Polyglot of Walton.

I would now, in all humility, in attempting so difficult a subject, confess my sense of frequent failure, and lack of ability sometimes to decide between the claims of different renderings. I trust, however, that the readers of this little book will deal to me a kindly criticism, as the translation was undertaken as a vacation-task, and the notes thrown together in the midst of various compulsory avocations.

May the Lord accept the feeble labours of His servant upon this portion of His inspired Scriptures, and make them instrumental in generating and quickening an interest in the mysteries of His Holy Word!

BATH, *March*, 1869.

# CONTENTS.

|  | PAGE |
|---|---|
| INTRODUCTION | xiii |
| CHAPTER I. | 1 |
| ,, II. | 7 |
| ,, III. | 18 |
| ,, IV. | 22 |
| ,, V. | 29 |
| ,, VI. | 35 |
| ,, VII. | 40 |
| ,, VIII. | 46 |
| ,, IX. | 54 |
| ,, X. | 60 |
| ,, XI. | 66 |
| ,, XII. | 72 |
| ,, XIII. | 78 |
| ,, XIV. | 85 |

# INTRODUCTION.

1. *Birth and family.*—Hosea (Saviour) was the son of Beeri, (my well.) When the name of a prophet's father is mentioned, according to Jewish criticism he is also to be esteemed a prophet. Nothing farther is known of his pedigree, except that there is a tradition of the rabbins that he was of the tribe of Issachar.

2. *Office.*—Hosea was a prophet to the ten tribes especially, although he does not forget to utter stern reproofs and warnings against, as well as predict future blessings to the two-tribe kingdom of Judah. It is worthy of notice that in his preface he mentions four kings of Judah, and but one of Israel. Some have inferred from this that he properly belonged to Judah, and was sent from Judah to denounce their coming doom to the kingdom of Israel; but it would rather appear from the internal evidence of his prophecies, that he regarded the kings of Judah only as belonging to the true and legitimate line of the royal succession, and that the schismatic separation of the ten tribes, with their man-appointed monarch, was abnormal and unrecognized by God. The king of Israel who is named seems only to have been introduced for the purpose of fixing the date of the prophecies with greater accuracy, and this partial honour may have been awarded to Jeroboam the Second, as he was the most noted of the line of Jehu, who had received a quasi-recognition of royal authority and a promise that his seed for four generations should occupy the primacy over the ten tribes, as a reward for his destruction of the ritual of Baal-worship out of Israel.

3. *The period of his prophesying* extended over a protracted period, which has been variously computed; all agree,

however, in assigning a long duration to our prophet's ministry. Hosea entered on his office in the time of Uzziah, king of Judah, but Uzziah was contemporary with Jeroboam of Israel for fourteen years, and survived him twenty-six years; we must, therefore, allot at the least these twenty-six years, with probably a margin of one or two years more, to include fairly a portion of Jeroboam's life-time. Jotham reigned sixteen years, and Ahaz the same period. In the sixth year of Hezekiah the prophecy of Hosea concerning the destruction of the ten-tribe kingdom was fulfilled, (2 Kings xviii. 10,) and as there is no mention of that occurrence in the book, it is but right to conclude that our prophet had departed this life before that crisis. Thus by allotting one or two years in this reign at the close of his career and the same narrow limit in that of Jeroboam the Second, king of Israel, at its commencement, the period of Hosea's official duties cannot be reckoned under a figure a little in excess of sixty years, extending from somewhere about 784 to 722 B.C. The contemporaneous kings of Israel were Jeroboam the Second, Zachariah, Shallum, Menahem, Pekahiah, Pekah, and Hoshea. In this length of life and service in his Master's cause he reminds us of Elisha, who prophesied for fifty years—of Daniel, who witnessed for God during the whole extent of the Babylonish captivity—of St. John, whose apostolic labours, at the lowest computation, equalled, if not considerably surpassed, those of our prophet—and of Polycarp, who at his martyrdom confessed before the proconsul, " Eighty and six years have I served the Lord." During this long tenure of office, it will be seen that Hosea was more or less contemporary with other members of " the goodly fellowship of the prophets"—Jonah and Amos, who probably entered on their office before him, and Isaiah, Micah, Joel, and Nahum, who were called subsequently to him.

4. *His special duties* were to preach against and oppose the idolatry of the calves, set up as symbols of Jehovah by Jeroboam the First, to whose name has ever been affixed that familiar but fearful title, " who made Israel to sin," but his mission did not end here. Baal-worship, the worship of

the sun and heavenly bodies, (Baalim,) and the planet Venus, (Astarte,) had been established as the national religion by Ahab and Jezebel; and although the outward worship of these gods had been demolished by Jehu, yet it was only destroyed on the surface—the ritual was gone, but the doctrine remained—the serpent was scotched but not killed; indeed it had rather assumed a more dangerous and deceptive form—" out of the serpent's root came forth a cockatrice "—they had put away the idol, but had transferred Jehovah to his pedestal, and treated the Lord of lords as though He had been like the gods of the heathen. They made images and dedicated them as similitudes of the Great Unseen; they worshipped Jehovah, but called Him Baali; they kept His feasts, but turned them into idol-revels. Against this mixture of holy and profane—this compromise, this latitudinarianism—against this degradation of the majesty of God by associating His presence with an idol-effigy—against this combination of revelation with the corruptions of heathenism—against these archaic prototypes of Rationalism and Romanism, Hosea was a preacher and a protestant.

*Style of composition.*—Hosea has ever been reckoned one of the most difficult of the Hebrew authors. His transitions are sharp and rapid, his connecting links few, his language abrupt and severe, and his figures tragic.

It may be doubted whether we have his prophecies in the full form in which they were at first delivered, or whether the writings preserved to us are an epitome of longer and more explicit announcements, as is probably the case in the speeches of SS. Peter, Stephen, and Paul, in the " Acts of the Apostles." This would account for some of the difficulties presented to us in the text—or they may be, without abridgment or omission, the *ipsissima verba* of our prophet, who gave utterance to these brief but comprehensive declarations at various and long separated periods of his ministry, in the sententious and oracular form in which we now possess them. In either case, the composition pictures the prophet to our mind's eye passing through the successive ages of man and the varied experiences of spiritual life. In all the zeal of youthful ardour and jealousy for his God, rising up as a reprover and reformer; in the fire of manhood denouncing the idolatries, iniquities, and impenitence of the nation,—the fruitful cause of all their present sufferings and future woe; and lastly, in the calm eventide of his old age, as the veil was yet further lifted up, gilding the far-distant future of his people with many a precious promise, like the setting sun, which, after a day of storm and tempest, breaks out from behind a barrier of thunder clouds, and darts a ray of light and glory across the scene of devastation, prophetic of a "morning without clouds."

The roll of Hosea is a "song of mercy and judgment." Throughout Israel's career of idolatry in former times, and continuance in unbelief in these latter days, his unfoldings reveal the sure and certain "tribulation and anguish" against "the Jew first;" and when they shall seek Jehovah their God, and Messiah their King, the "glory, honour, and peace" that are in reversion, "to the Jew first." To the backslider also amongst ourselves the same message comes home, charged alike with reproof and reprieve. Whether, therefore, we regard the contents of this book in their proper, primary, and literal reference to the nation of Israel, or make an application of them, in a figure, to the present necessities of the Church of God, we may well lay to heart the parting words of the aged and honoured prophet—

"Who is wise, then shall he understand these things;
(Who is) understanding, then shall he know them;
For righteous are the ways of Jehovah,
And the just shall walk in them,
But transgressors shall fall in them."

# The Book of the Prophet Hosea.

### Chapter I.

1   The word of Jehovah, which was to Hoshea,¹ the son of Beeri, in the days² of Uzziah, Jotham, Ahaz, Hezekiah, kings of Judah; and in the days of Jeroboam, son of Joash, king of Israel.

2   The beginning of Jehovah's speaking through³ Hoshea;

Then said Jehovah to Hoshea,
Go, take to thyself a wife of wantonness,⁴

1.   ¹ " Hosea " = salvation. "Beeri" = my well. These names, like others in this prophet, are symbolical.

² " In the days of," &c. For the duration of the period of Hosea's prophetic office, see Introduction, p. xiii. § 3.

2.   ³ " Through Hosea"—literally " in "—the Spirit spoke in his heart. This form ב, דבר, is used frequently of divine communications, and is probably intended to show the indwelling of the inspiring Spirit, and His energizing influences in the prophet's heart and mind. (See Num. xii. 6, 8; Hab. ii. 1; Zech. i. 9, &c.)

⁴ "A wife of wantonness"—literally " of fornications." The difficulty of this passage has been felt by all commentators, on account of its apparent violation of a divine command, (Deut. xxii. 21.) The leading interpretations are these:—

(1)   That it was an outward and literal act, the law being set aside by the command of the Legislator Himself.

And children of wantonness,
Because the אֶרֶץ hath utterly played the wanton,
Instead of (following) after Jehovah.

3   And he went, and took Gomer,[5] the daughter of Diblaim; and she conceived and bare him a son.
4   Then said Jehovah to him,

אֵלָיו יְהוָה וַיֹּאמֶר

(2) That the transaction was not real, but performed in a vision.

(3) That the sin spoken of is used figuratively, to represent a forsaking of God and an union with idols; that the whole nation had become " wantons " in this sense, and Hosea in consequence was simply told to marry a wife of this unfaithful people, and beget children who should be guilty of the same defection.

(4) That nothing more is meant than a foreign wife—one not of the holy nation, but of the polluted heathen.

The best way of arriving at a safe conclusion in a difficulty like this, is to consider what is required by the fact to be represented in the figure, and to rule accordingly. Israel is pictured as a wanton wife, and her children or people as of like character; but Israel was chosen in purity, and her wantonness and adultery against God were sins that followed her calling. She left her first husband, and fell into sin. Then the mercy of God is represented in His taking her back after her disgrace. Hence it may be concluded that Gomer was not a disreputable person when Hosea took her, any more than her children which were yet unborn, but was guilty of defection afterwards, and the names " wife and children of wantonness " are given as the result of foreknowledge. This explanation obviates the difficulty of the literal view, and introduces no fancy or force-work into the text.

3.   [5] " Gomer " = completion—the filling up the measure of iniquity. " Diblaim " = a double cake of figs—emblematic of the luxury and self-indulgence of sin.

## CHAPTER I.

קְרָא שְׁמוֹ יִזְרְעֶאל
Call his name Jezreel,[6]
Because yet a little while, יִזְרְעֶאל
And I will visit the blood of Jezreel[7] upon the
house of Jehu,

יְהוּא עַל־בֵּית

4. [6] "Jezreel." There is a paranomasia between this word and Israel. Israel had become Jezreel. Jezreel has two meanings:—(1) "God shall scatter;" (2) "God shall sow." Thus the one word binds up in itself the curse and the blessing—the dispersion and the restoration. The context decides (as will be seen) the sense which is intended in each case. With reference to the mother, the personification of the nation, Israel is scattered because of their iniquities, but beloved for the fathers' sakes, and so when God's purposes are ripe, the punished shall be pardoned, and the banished restored; Jezreel the "scattered," shall become Jezreel the "sown" again in their own land. We have a similar instance in the name Isaac, (laughter,) which comprises the two opposite ideas—the smile of the sceptic, and the happiness of the rejoicing saint. Sarah's laugh of unbelief at the annunciation of his birth has found an echo in the infidel scoffs of her posterity; and the laughter of joy at his birth, on the other hand, shall yet find its antitype when the Lord shall make "Jerusalem a rejoicing, and her people a joy."

[7] The interpretations of "the blood of Jezreel" are various:—

(1) The blood of Jezreel signifies the blood of Ahab's family, shed by Jehu, (see 2 Kings ch. x.;) for though the slaughter was commanded by God, yet the act was executed by Jehu for his own ends.—*Calvin. Pusey.*

(2) The various acts of cruelty committed by Jehu at Jezreel.—*Newcome.*

(3) Jezreel refers not to the place but to Hosea's son, and represents the godly seed, of which Jehu's posterity, being idolaters, were persecutors.—*Horsley.*

וחיה 5  
בעמק  
ויאמר  
קרא שמה  
ארחם

And I will put an end to ישראל  
The ממלכות⁸ of the בית of Israel.  
5 And it shall be in that day;  
That I will break the bow of Israel  
In the valley of Jezreel.⁹ יזרעאל  
6 And she conceived again, and bare a daughter,  
And He said to him, לו  
Call her name Lo-ruhamah; לא רחמה [*not pitied*]  
Because I will not again pity the house of Israel,  
But I will utterly take away את־בית אח ישראל  
(The kingdoms) that belong to them.  
להם

(4) It would seem that Hosea's son Jezreel is pointed at in this place, and inasmuch as he has just been described as a son of wantonness, he could not represent the godly seed, but the idolatrous people of the nation. Now Jehu and his family had been raised to the throne to extirpate these rebels against God; but after having executed a great slaughter, Jehu and his sons fell into equally gross idolatry, therefore the blood they shed to no purpose was required at their hands.

⁸ "Kingdoms." The original is plural, and should be so rendered, as Israel's kingdom was constantly changing the line of succession in its rulers.

5. ⁹ "Jezreel,"—here the noted valley, or plain of Esdraelon, where it would seem that, as being the scene of frequent battles, the last decisive victory was won over Hoshea, the last king of Israel.

6. ¹⁰ "I will utterly take away," &c. Some render, "that I should ever be forgiving them;" *i.e.*, taking away their iniquity, (so Jun. and Trem., Houbigant, Horsley, &c.) Pusey, "I will take away everything from them." It seems preferable to supply the object of the verb from the fourth verse, "kingdoms," and render as in the text.

LXX., ἀντιτασσόμενος ἀντιτάξομαι αὐτοῖς. "I will utterly

## CHAPTER I.  5

7 But the house of Judah I will pity,
  And will save them by Jehovah¹¹ their God;
  And will not save them by bow, nor by sword,
    nor by battle,
  By horses, nor by horsemen.

8 And she weaned Lo-ruhamah; and conceived, and
    bare a son.

9 And He said,
  Call his name Lo-Ammi;    [*not my people*]
  For ye (are) not my people,
  And I (am) not "I am"¹² to you.

oppose them." Syr., "Eos penitus ablaturus." The Vulg.
reads נשא, "Oblivione obliviscar eorum," "I will utterly
forget them." Targum, "Dimittendo dimittam eis."

7. ¹¹ "By Jehovah their God." This is a strong testimony
to the Deity of the Messiah, and was so felt to be by the
Chaldee paraphrast, who renders במימרא דיי, "by the Word
of the Lord." And if we take the destruction of Sennache-
rib's army (2 Kings xix. 35) to be the primary fulfilment
of this prophecy, it is a striking coincidence that that
deliverance was wrought by the Angel of Jehovah—the
Word of God. We look, however, for a future and exhaustive fulfilment of the promise, when the Lord shall
smite the Antichrist; and Israel, at present personified by
Lo-ruhamah, shall become Ruhamah, and welcome her
returning King with the predicted greeting, "Blessed is He
that cometh in the name of the Lord."

9. ¹² "Not 'I am,'" לא־אהיה לכם. Houbigant suggests
the reading אלהיכם, "your God," but such alterations are
more ingenious than profitable. There seems rather to be a
reference to Exodus iii., where, in the 7th verse, God avouches
Israel to be His people, and in the 14th verse gives Moses a
command to announce to them His covenant-name, as a

ground of confidence to them, " I Am (אהיה) hath sent me unto you." Now, however, their sins have separated between them and their God, and the Lord threatens them with desertion and rescinding of His covenant.

This interpretation is strengthened by the fact that Lo-ammi is treated as one title; so also Lo-Eh'yeh must be viewed in the same light.

LXX., Καὶ ἐγὼ οὐκ εἰμὶ ὑμῶν. Vulg., " Ego non ero vester." Syr., " Nec ego futurus sum vester." Targum, מימרי לא הוה בסעדיכון, " Verbum meum non erit in adjutorium vestrum," " My Word shall not be your help."

With this verse the first chapter in the Hebrew text ends.

## Chapter II. (Heb.)

1 Yet shall the number of the sons of Israel be like the sand of the sea,
Which cannot be measured, and cannot be numbered,
And it shall be in the place that it was said to them Lo-ammi are ye,
It shall be said unto them,
Sons of the living God (are ye).[1]

1. [1] The darkest period of night is that immediately before day-break, and so out of the darkest affliction rises the morning star of promise.

Much interest has been attached to this verse on account of its citation by St. Paul, in Rom. ix. 25, and St. Peter, in his first epistle, ii. 10, where the general impression is that the words in question are interpreted by the apostles as referring to the Gentiles and not to Israel, and hence an argument has been deduced for the general transference of all the prophecies which detail the hopes and destinies of Israel, in a figure, to the Christian Church, or to the Gentiles. Let us glance at the two quotations in order.

(1) In Rom. ix. St. Paul is speaking of the election of God as manifested in the call of both Jews and Gentiles. His words are, (verses 22—26,) "What if God, willing to show His wrath, and to make His power known, endured with much longsuffering the vessels of wrath fitted to destruction: and that He might make known the riches of His glory on the vessels of mercy, which He had afore prepared unto glory, even us, whom He hath called, not of the Jews only, but also of the Gentiles? As He saith also in Osee, I will call them my people, which were not my people; and her beloved, which was not beloved. And it shall come to pass, that in the place where it was said unto them, ye are not my people; there shall they be called the children of the living God."

2 And gathered shall be the sons of Judah and the sons of Israel together,

Nothing further can surely be inferred from this place than that the Apostle quotes these words as apposite to the case before him; just as Israel, through unbelief, ceased to be God's people, yet "a remnant according to the election of grace" was recovered, restored, and owned of God; just so has it fallen out with the Gentiles also, " God hath visited the Gentiles to take out of them a people for His name." The "also" in verse 25 supports this view. Thus Israel in this point also furnishes a type and pattern. God's dealings with them are our lesson-book, to teach us His plans and purposes with reference to the world at large. Their experiences have been preserved to us as a miniature portrait of some noted ancestor, in which we may trace the same stamp and resemblance throughout all the posterity of the family of grace.

(2.) St. Peter's quotation is not encumbered with any real difficulty. It is the opinion of most commentators that his epistles were addressed to mixed congregations of Jews and Gentiles, but this and other passages referred to in proof of this theory, shew clearly that he was writing to Jews only. The apostle, in his preface, dedicates his first epistle to the "strangers scattered abroad," παρεπιδήμοις διασπορᾶς, literally "strangers of the dispersion." This word, διασπορά, " dispersion," is set apart in Scripture for Jewish reference; it always means that nation, and never the Gentiles. The eighteenth verse of chap. i., where the phrase occurs, "The vain conversation received by tradition from your fathers," is pointed out as a Gentile reference, but surely no more exact parallel could be produced than these words supply to the rebuke so frequent on the lips of the Lord, against the *traditions* of the Scribes and Pharisees, by which they had made the word of God of none effect. Again, chapter ii. 9, the verse that precedes the quotation under discussion, reminds them of the high and holy vocation of the Hebrew nation, registered in

## CHAPTER II.

And shall appoint to them one head,²
the Pentateuch, (see Ex. xix. 5, 6,) "ראש אחד Ye are a chosen generation, a royal priesthood, an holy nation, a peculiar people." And the words of Hosea follow on this reminder of their pristine glory, to show them how they had in time past fallen from the pedestal of Divine favour, but now again, through faith in the Gospel of the Messiah, they who received the grace of God had been replaced and re-established in their ancient privilege and prerogative. And in verse 12 the distinction between them and the Gentiles is again pointedly marked, "Having your conversation honest among the Gentiles." The form of this sentence, it will be observed, is very different from a parallel one of St. Paul, when he writes to a Gentile Church in a similar vein—"This I say therefore, and testify in the Lord, that ye walk not as other (τὰ λοιπά) Gentiles walk," (Eph. iv. 17.) St. Peter's converts are distinguished as a nation both by extraction and calling; St. Paul's by calling only. The reader may also be reminded that St. Peter, after he had opened the door to both Jews and Gentiles at Jerusalem and Cæsarea, was set apart to the apostleship of the circumcision; and the fact that this epistle was written at Babylon, (ch. v. 13,) notwithstanding the tradition of Jerome and the Church of Rome, is an evidence that he was employed in that department of the great mission field. There seems, therefore, to be no ground from the use made of our prophet's language by the two apostles, to favour the unscriptural idea that Israel is ever to be confounded with the Gentiles, or because we have been made partakers with them of the promises through being engrafted into their olive tree, (Rom. xi. 17,) that therefore we are to usurp their place, and thrust them out of the goodly and glorious inheritance which the Lord has been pleased to reveal in His word as designed and destined for them in the latter day.

2. ² "One head," ראש אחד. This prophecy might

And shall go up from the land;
Because great (shall be) the day of Jezreel.¹

CHAPTER II. (Eng. ver.)

3  Say ye to your brethren, Ammi;  [*my people*]
   And to your sisters, Ru-hamah.⁴  [*pitied one*]
4  Strive with your mother,⁵ strive ye,
   Because as for her, she is not my wife,

receive a partial fulfilment under Zerubbabel, when many of the ten tribes returned with the two, but the grandeur and completeness of the salvation predicted, and the reversal of all their woes, point to one greater than he. " From the land," *i.e.*, of their captivity ; " from all nations whither I have driven them."

LXX., ἀρχὴν μίαν. Syr., "Principem unum." Vulg., "Caput unum." Targum, ריש חד מן בית דוד, " Principem unum de domo David."

³ " Jezreel," here " God shall sow." Great shall be the day of Israel's restoration and recovery—" life from the dead "— the conversion of the heathen — the establishment of the kingdom.

3. ⁴ Mark the punishments of Israel, typified in the symbolic names, are turned into blessings. Jezreel, " God shall scatter," is now Jezreel," God shall sow ; " Lo-ammi, " not my people," avouched to be Ammi, " my people ;" and Lo-ruhamah, " the unpitied and unloved," Ruhamah, " the pitied, loved, and adopted for ever." Thus, before entering on the dirge of the now opening roll of prophecy, the Lord unfolds all the tenderness of His heart to win to repentance and faith in Him. The first-fruits of the fulfilment of this prophecy were gathered at the first advent of Messiah, the harvest shall be garnered at His second appearing and kingdom.

4. ⁵ " Your mother," *i.e.*, Gomer, the personification of the kingdom of the ten tribes.

And as for myself, I am not her husband;
That she may put away her wantonness from her face,
And her adulteries from between her breasts.
5 Lest I strip her stark-naked,
And expose her,
As on the day she was born;
And render her like the wilderness,
And make her like a land of drought,
And put her to death with thirst.
6 And her children I will not pity;
Because children of wantonness are they.
7 Because their mother hath played the wanton,
She hath caused them shame⁶ that conceived them;
Because she said,
I will go after my lovers,⁷
Who give (me) my bread and my water,
My wool and my flax,

ריבו. LXX., κρίθητε. Aq. and Symm., εἰκάσασθε. Syr., "Contendite." Vulg., "Judicate." Targ., "Arguite."

5. The figures in this verse are gathered from the period of Israel's earliest history. The day of her birth as a nation, was when she was brought out of Egypt, naked and defenceless as an infant, and the threat that the Lord would reduce her to a similar state of want and suffering, is clothed in language borrowed from the "waste and howling wilderness," with its drought and desolation.

7. ⁶ "Hath caused them shame." The full force of the Hiphil הובישה is to be retained, as LXX., κατῄσχυνεν. The Syr., Vulg., and Targum, however, take it passively.

⁷ "My lovers," מאהבי. Used of the idols who were Israel's paramours, that tempted her to act unfaithfully towards God.

My oil, and my wines.⁸

8 Therefore, behold, I will block up thy way⁹ with thorns;
And I will rear up a wall,
And her paths she shall not find.

9 And she shall pursue her lovers and not overtake them,
And shall seek them and not find (them);
Then shall she say,
I will go and return to my former husband,
For it was better with me then, than (it is) now.

10 But as for her, she knew not,
That it was I, that gave her,
The corn, and the must, and the oil;
And silver I multiplied to her, and gold,
They made (it) into a Baal.¹⁰

---

⁸ "My wines," שיקויי. LXX., πάντα ὅσα μοι καθήκει. Syr., "Quicquid mihi necessarium est." Vulg., "Potum meum." Targ., כל פרנוסי, "Omnia alimenta mea." The state of things here pourtrayed points to the prosperity of the nation under Jeroboam II. (See 2 Kings xiv. 25—28.)

8. ⁹ "Thy way," דרכך. LXX., τὴν ὁδὸν αὐτῆς, "her way." And so the Syriac. The Vulg. and Targum, follow the Hebrew text.

10. ¹⁰ "They made it into a Baal," עשו לבעל. Ahab having married Jezebel, daughter of the king of Zidon, reintroduced the worship of Baal (see Judges ii. 11, &c.)— probably the sun—into Israel. They made sun-images in honour of Baal out of the gold with which God had enriched them. So the Targum and Syriac expound it. This translation is far more suited to the general drift of the passage than the tame rendering, "they offered the gold to Baal."

LXX., ἐποίησε τῇ Βάαλ. Syr., "Ex quo confecerunt

11 Therefore I will return,
And take back my corn in its time,
And my must in its season;
And I will pluck away my wool and my flax,
(Given) to cover her nakedness.
12 And now, I will uncover her vileness before the eyes of her lovers;
And no man shall pluck her out of my hand.
13 And I will put an end to her every joy,
Her feast, her new moon and her sabbath;
And her every festival.
14 And I will lay waste her vine, and her fig-tree,
Of which she said,
A love-fee are these to me,
Which they gave to me (even) my lovers;
But I will make them into a forest,
And devour them shall the beast of the field.
15 And I will visit upon her
The days of the Baals,[11] to whom she burned incense,
And decked her with her nose-ring and her necklace.
And went after her lovers;
But ME she forgat, declareth Jehovah.[12]

Baalem." Vulg., "Quo fecerunt Baal." Targum, מניה, "Ex quo."

15. [11] "The days of the Baals"—the shameful feast-days in honour of their idols.

[12] "Declareth," נאֻם; properly a participial noun, from נאם. Compare the Latin "fatum," a "solemn declaration," an "oracle." This word is never used absolutely, but is always followed by the Author of the revelation made. In almost every instance it is employed to express the immediate utterance of the Divine Being, and it furnishes therefore

16 Therefore, behold, I myself do entice her,
And cause her to go to the wilderness,
And I will speak to her heart.

17 And I will give her her vineyards (when she cometh) from thence,
And the valley of Achor to be a door of hope;[13]
And she shall sing anthems[14] there as in the days of her youth,

a strong attestation of the doctrine of inspiration. Our Lord fixed His seal to the true import of this word when about to quote the first verse of Psalm cx., where it occurs, "David himself *said by the Holy Ghost.*" (See Mark xii. 36.) In Num. xxiv. 3, 4, 15, 16; 2 Sam. xxiii. 1; and Prov. xxx. 1, נאם is followed by a human speaker, but the purport of each of these places seems to require that it should be interpreted as a Divine oracle or revelation received by the speaker from the Spirit of God. One passage of great difficulty occurs in Psalm xxxvi. 1, where, out of the many modes of expounding the opening words, that seems to be best which interprets them as " a revelation made by God to David's heart concerning the wickedness of the wicked." The word is found also in verses 18 and 3, and in chap. xi. 11, of our prophet.

17. [13] " For a door of hope," לפתח תקוה. When Israel first entered Canaan the valley of Achor was a scene of trouble and defeat, on account of Achan's deceit and pelf, (see Josh. vii.;) but on her second coming to the land of promise, there shall be no Achan to bring down God's judgment, and no defeat from any foe, but " a hope " of everlasting possession that shall " not make ashamed."

LXX., διανοῖξαι σύνεσιν αὐτῆς. Symm., εἰς θύραν ἐλπίδος. Theod., ἀνεῴξασθαι τὴν ὑπομονὴν αὐτῆς. Syr., " Ut aperiatur intellectus ejus." Vulg., " Ad aperiendam spem." Targum, להחמודי נפש, " Ad delicias animæ."

[14] " Sing anthems," ענתה. This translation seems most

And as in the day she came up from the land of Egypt.

18  And it shall be in that day, declareth Jehovah,
That thou shalt call me Ishi,     [*my husband*]
And thou shalt not call me any more Baali.[15]
                               [*my Baal, or lord*]
19  And I will remove the names of the Baals, out of her mouth;
And they shall not be remembered any more by their name.
20  And I will make for them a covenant in that day
With the beast of the field, and with the fowl of the air,
And the reptile of the ground;
And the bow and the sword and the battle I will break from off the land,

appropriate, because the word really implies "answering," which points to the antiphonal character of the song of triumph, as in the song of Miriam, (Ex. xv.,) referred to in this verse. It will be seen below that several of the ancient translators took this verb in the sense of humiliation.

LXX., ταπεινωθήσεται.    Symm., κακωθήσεται.    Theod., ἀποκριθήσεται.   Syr., "Humilietur."   Vulg., "Canet."   Targ., "Dedent sese ibi verbo meo."

18. [15] The word "Baali," originally meaning "lord," or "master," had been improperly applied to the idol. The word had been prostituted, and God would not reclaim it to His service. He would be called Ishi, "my husband"— אִישׁ; literally, "a man." It is possible that the humanity of the Messiah, the God-man, is also here referred to. (See Zech. vi. 12, and John xix. 5.)

בְּעָלִי. LXX., Βααλείμ. Aquila, ἔχων με. Vulg., "Baali." So also the Syriac. Targum, "Non servietis ultra idolis populorum."

     And will cause them to rest in security.
21  And I will espouse thee to myself for ever;
     And I will espouse thee to myself with justice
       and judgment,
     And with grace and much pity.
22  And I will espouse[16] thee to myself with fidelity;
     And thou shalt know Jehovah.
23  And it shall be in that day
     I will answer, declareth Jehovah,
     I will answer the heavens;
     And they shall answer the earth,
24  And the earth shall answer
     The corn, and the must and the oil;
     And they shall answer Jezreel.[17]
25  And I will sow her to myself in the land,
     And will pity Lo-ruhamah;    [*the not pitied*]
     And I will say to Lo-ammi, Ammi art thou,
          [*not my people;  my people*]
     And he shall say, my God![18]

22. [16] The thrice-repeated use of the tender word "betroth," reveals to us the love and longing of God towards His people. This threefold repetition also, taken in connection with the several modes and manifestations of the Divine love associated with each, must have a tacit reference, as is so frequently the case in the Old Testament Scriptures, to the doctrine of the Trinity.

24. [17] "Jezreel" is here used in the good sense, associated with a promise of future blessings, "God shall sow," as the next verse proves.

25. [18] Observe, the reconciliation comes from God, as in Zech. xiii. 9. From Him must flow forth to us preventing grace, that we may have a good will, as well as working with

us when we have that good will. (Article X.) Here God renews the covenant of Ex. iii., which He had suspended in ch. i. 9, of our prophet. Now the God of Israel, who had so long hidden Himself, returns to them, and they, acted upon by His grace and love, return to Him. God and Israel are reconciled, and with Israel, all His people, children of Abraham by faith. The promise of Immanuel is thus verified. The source of happiness before the fall was that God was with man; the prophecy of restoration to that forfeited blessing through the coming Messiah was uttered by Isaiah— " Behold, a virgin shall conceive and bear a son, and shall call his name Immanuel." The evangelist records the fulfilment of this prediction, when Christ took our nature upon Him, and dwelt on earth, and furnishes the interpretation, " God with us;" and in Rev. xxi. 3, we have the full and final exhaustion of the same promise, expressed in the expansion of the blessed name, καὶ αὐτὸς ὁ Θεὸς μετ' αὐτῶν ἔσται, αὐτῶν Θεός, "And He Himself shall be God with them—their God."

## Chapter III.

1 אָמַר יְהוָֹה אֵלַי
Then said Jehovah to me,
אֱהַב־אִשָּׁה Again go, love the woman,[1]
אֲהֲבַת Loved of her spouse,[2] though an adulteress;
כְּאַהֲבַת Like as the love of Jehovah for the sons of Israel,
For they turn after strange gods,
And are lovers of cakes of grapes.[3]

2 And I bought[4] her to myself for fifteen silverlings,
and a homer of barley, and a lethek of barley.

1. [1] "The *woman*"—evidently the same Gomer who, according to the first chapter, was to be a wife of wantonness. She had gone astray from Hosea, and he was now commanded, in order to carry out the figure of God's mercy on a spiritually adulterous people, to love her again, and forgive her defection.

[2] "Spouse," רֵעַ.—literally, friend or neighbour—but as Hosea her husband is intended, I have used the word "spouse," though perhaps rather too strong a title, as the original seems rather to point out the fact that the wife did not deserve the husband's affection, by using a far less affectionate word than אִישׁ, "husband."

אֲהֲבַת רֵעַ. LXX., ἀγαπῶσαν πονηρά. And so Syriac, "Amantem scelera;" reading רָע. Vulg., "Dilectam amico." Targ., "Qui similes sunt mulieri charissimæ suo marito."

[3] "Cakes of grapes"—offered to idols. Some render "flagons of wine," but see versions quoted below. Hengstenberg derives it from אֵשׁ, "fire;" Henderson, from אָשַׁשׁ, to "press."

אֲשִׁישֵׁי. LXX., Πέμματα σταφίδος. Aq., Παλαιά. Symm., Ἀκάρπους. Syr., "Macerata uvarum passarum." Vulg., "Vinacia uvarum."

2. [4] "I bought," וָאֶכְּרֶהָ. Hengstenberg's interpretation of this word is doubtless the true one, (see "Christology," vol. i., 189;) the verb כרה signifies to dig, and the reference

## CHAPTER III.

וָאֹמַר 3  And I said to her, אֵלֶיהָ
יָמִים     Many days shalt thou wait for me, תֵּשְׁבִי
            Thou shalt not play the wanton,
            And thou shalt not become (subject) to (any) man;
            And I also (will wait) for thee.
יָמִים 4  Because many days
יִשְׂרָאֵל    Shall the sons of Israel wait,
            (They shall have) no king, and no prince, אֵין מֶלֶךְ וְאֵין שַׂר
וְאֵין זֶבַח    And no sacrifice, and no statue, זֶבַח וּמַצֵּבָה
            And no ephod, nor teraphim.⁵
            וְהַרָפִים אֵפוֹד אֵין

here is to the digging or boring the ear of a slave. The figure then is perfect. She had forfeited her claims, by joining herself to paramours. Hosea redeemed her for the price of a slave, thirty shekels of silver, half he paid in money and half in kind; and then he bored her ear, fixed her as his for ever; hence she was to wait long for him. Just so the Lord is now dealing with Israel. He has bored their ears to be His servants, His witnesses, willingly or unwillingly, and they must wait many days for Him, till He reveals Himself at His second advent, and they acknowledge Him as Lord and God.

For the second שְׂעֹרִים, the LXX., Symm., and Theod., read οἴνου. Vulg., "hordei." Syr., renders whole clause by "sesquimodio hordei."

4. ⁵ A remarkable prophecy, and remarkably fulfilled before our eyes. Israel has no king, and no prince of the captivity, known to be the heir of the throne, though kept from his rights by foreign dominion. They have no true and lawful worship according to the Mosaic code, neither have they any unlawful or idolatrous worship, for both the service of God and that of idols are designated in the following words. They have no sacrifice appointed by God, for those only could be offered at Jerusalem; they have no statue, no great public idol, like the Calves or Baal. They have no ephod, in

c 2

5  Afterwards, shall the sons of Israel return,
יִשְׂרָאֵל בְּנֵי
And seek Jehovah their God, אֱלֹהֵיהֶם
אֶת־יְהֹוָה
And David⁶ their king;
וְדָוִיד

which were the Urim and Thummim, which in former days revealed to them the will of God on the occasion of any particular difficulty; nor have they teraphim, "penates," "household gods," to consult on an emergency, according to the magical rites of the heathen. These words refer especially, it may be noted, to the ten tribes, and may lead us either to reject every theory of their supposed discovery, or to conclude that they returned after the Babylonish captivity, with the two tribes, and thus that the prophecy points to the whole twelve-tribe people, known now as Jews all over the world.

See, for an excellent comment on this verse, Dr. M'Caul's Act Sermon before the University of Dublin.

For מצבה, "statue," two MSS. read מנחה, "offering."

אין אפוד ותרפים. LXX., Οὐδὲ ἱερατείας οὐδὲ δήλων. Symm. and Theod., ἄνευ Ἐφὼδ καὶ ἄνευ Θεραφίμ. The Codex Barberinus, however, Aquila, καὶ μορφωμάτων. Symm., οὐδὲ ἐπιλύσεως. Theod., οὐδὲ ἐπιλυομένου. Syr., "Sine induente ephod et adolente thura." Vulg., "Sine ephod et sine teraphim." Targum, "Nec non ephod, nec qui responsum reddat."

5. ⁶ "David" = Messiah. We are not to regard this name as a patronymic, as some have done, denoting the line of David's successors, nor suppose that another king will rise who shall bear that name, but must rather investigate the meaning of the symbolic name itself. David, signifies "beloved," and when our Lord was baptized, and entered, so to speak, on His spiritual supremacy, the voice from Heaven proclaimed Him as the "Beloved Son," the "David" that should come. Again, at the Transfiguration, when the Lord revealed the coming kingdom with its heavenly manifestations and earthly glory, the same proclamation was

## CHAPTER III.

אֶל־יְהוָֹה וּפָחֲדוּ And revere⁷ Jehovah
וְאֶל־טוּבוֹ And His gracious one⁸
בְּאַחֲרִית הַיָּמִים In the last days.

announced from the excellent glory—"This is my beloved Son," the true David; "hear Him!" He is your King, obey His voice!

⁷ "Revere," literally, tremble to— אֶל. It shall not be a fear that repels, but a fear, a holy fear, that attracts.

⁸ "His Gracious One," טוּבוֹ, here, from the parallelism epexegetical, "of David their King," hence "Gracious," or "Good One," is a synonym of Messiah. Compare, for the radical passage, Ex. xxxiii. 19. (See ch. viii. 3, and xiv. 3,) &c., &c.

פחדו אל וב'. LXX., ἐκστήσονται ἐπὶ τῷ κυρίῳ καὶ ἐπὶ τοῖς ἀγαθοῖς αὐτοῦ. Vulg., "Pavebunt ad dominum et ad bonum ejus." Syr., "Et cognoscent dominum et bonitatem ejus." Targum, "Studebunt cultui Domini et multiplicabitur bonitas ejus."

## CHAPTER IV.

1 HEAR ye the word of Jehovah, O sons of Israel;
For Jehovah hath a strife[1] with the inhabitants of the land,
Because (there is) no truth and no mercy,
And no knowledge of God in the land.

2 Swearing and lying,
And murdering and thieving, and committing adultery (are there);
They have burst forth,[2]
And blood with blood[3] commingleth.

3 Therefore mourn shall the land,
And faded shall be every inhabitant of it,
The very beast of the field, and the fowl[4] of the air,
And also the fish of the sea shall perish.

1. [1] "Strife." A judicial enquiry and cause.

2. [2] "They have burst forth." They have broken through all laws, as a swollen river bursts its banks. Every commandment they have violated.

[3] "Blood with blood." The usual exposition of these words is that murders were so frequent that the streams of blood flowed into each other. The sin of incest seems rather to be referred to, as the climax of adultery, the last abomination mentioned. This seems to be clearly the interpretation of the Targum.

LXX., καὶ αἵματα ἐφ' αἵμασι μίσγουσι. Vulg., "Et sanguis sanguinem tetigit." Syr., "Et sanguinem cum sanguine commiscuerunt." Targ., the whole passage, "Et adulteria committentes generant filios ex uxoribus proximorum suorum, et aggregant peccata peccatis."

3. [4] "The very beast and the fowl," בחית — בעוף. It is best to consider the ב in these words as the ב essentiæ, and to render "the very beast," &c. Thus the Syriac, "Tum bestiæ, tum volucres," &c.

## CHAPTER IV.

4   Yet let no man strive with,
    Nor rebuke another;
    And (let not) thy people (be)
    Strivers with the priest.⁵
5   For thou shalt fall by day,
    And fall shall the prophet also with thee by night;
    And I will annihilate⁶ thy mother.⁷

4. ⁵ "The priest," throughout Hosea, seems to mean the idolatrous priests, who led the people astray. The ordinary translation will therefore scarcely be consistent. By repeating the imperative contained in the first clause in the second, we obtain the following result. Though the whole nation is gone astray, let no man reprove his neighbour on this account; nay, more, let not the whole people arise and rebuke the idolatrous priests, for (see following verse) the Lord will take the matter into His own hands. The כ in כמריבי is the כ *veritatis*, and not כ *comparationis*. (See Num. xi. 1.)

כמריבי כהן. LXX., ὁ δὲ λαός μου ὡς ἀντιλεγόμενος ἱερεύς. Vulg., "Populus enim tuus, sicut hi qui contradicunt sacerdoti." Syr., "Populus tuus æque ac sacerdos contendit." Targum, "Populus vero tuus litigat cum doctoribus suis."

5. ⁶ "Annihilate." This verb is variously rendered. LXX., ὡμοίωσα, "I made like." Vulg., "Tacere feci," "I have brought to silence." Syr., "Conticuit." Targum, "Confusione induam congregationem vestram."

⁷ "Thy mother." Commentators are divided. Some regard the mother-country, the Israelitish state, to be intended; others the mother-city, and then a question arises as to whether Jerusalem or Samaria, the capital of the ten tribes, is meant. Surely, although the Israelitish nationality may lie in the background, the term "mother" clearly points to Gomer, (ch. i. 3.)

6  Annihilated are my people through lack of (true) knowledge;  [lit., *the knowledge*]
Because thou (true) knowledge hast rejected,
I also have rejected thee from being priest to me,
And (because) thou hast forgotten the law of thy God,
I will forget thy sons,—even I myself.
7  According as they increased,
So they sinned against me;
Their glory
Into shame will I turn.
8  The sin-offering [8] of my people
They devour;
And upon their iniquity [9]
They each do set their lust.
9  And the people shall be like the priest;
And I will visit upon them their ways,
And their actions will I requite to them.
10  And they shall eat, and not be satisfied,
They have played the wanton, but shall not increase;
For Jehovah they have forsaken

---

8. [8] "Sin-offering." The priests desire that my people may sin, that they may have abundance of sacrifices to feast on.

[9] "And upon their iniquity," &c. They lift their soul or desire, *i.e.*, they have a greedy appetite for the offerings which are then brought in consequence of their iniquity. Literally, they lift—his soul. The suffix "his" shows the sin of each individual priest, as the nominative "they" the universality of the sin. A few MSS. and LXX., Syr., Targ., Vulg., and Arab., read however, נפשם, *their* souls.

With respect to regarding (Him).[10]
11  Wantonness and wine and must
    Take possession of (their) heart.[11]
12  As for my people, their stock[12] they enquire of,
    And their staff declares to them;
    Because the spirit of wantonness hath led (them) astray,
    And they have played the wanton by departing from their God.   [lit., *from under their God*]
13  On the tops of the mountains they sacrifice,
    And on the hills they burn incense,
    Under the oak and the aspen and the terebinth,
    Because their shade is good;
    Therefore, your daughters shall play the wanton,
    And your brides shall commit adultery.
14  I will not punish your daughters because they play the wanton,
    Nor your brides because they commit adultery,
    Because they themselves with harlots go astray,

10. [10] Horsley proposes to alter the accentuation, and join "to regard" with the next verse, but such an alteration would not be in accordance with Hebrew idiom, as the verb שמר is not found connected with such objects as "wantonness," "wine," or the like.

11. [11] The LXX. translators make "the heart" the subject, and the other nouns the object. The Syr., Vulg., and Targum support the order of the text.

12. [12] "Stock"—an idol of wood. "Staff," perhaps bearing on it the carving of some idol, or the expression may point to the ancient superstition of Rhabdomancy, or the divination by rods.

And with prostitutes they sacrifice;
Therefore the people shall not understand,
They shall be overthrown.
15 Though thou playest the wanton, O Israel,
Let not Judah be guilty;
And come ye not to Gilgal,
And go not up to Beth-aven,[13]
And swear ye not " Jehovah liveth."
16 Because like a restive heifer,
Restive has been Israel,
Now shall Jehovah feed them,
Like a sheep in a wide space.
17 A companion of idols is Ephraim,
Leave (him) to himself.[14]

15. [13] "Bethel," the house of God, had become through the idolatry of the calves, "Beth-aven," the house of vanity, or idols.
LXX., οἶκον Ὤν. Aquila and Theod., οἶκον ἀνωφελῆ. Symm., οἶκον ἀδείας. In the Codex Barberinus, Aquila, Symm., and Theod., οἶκον ἀνωφελοῦς. Syr. and Vulg., "Bethaven." Targum, "Bethel."
17. [14] "Leave (him) to himself," הנח־לו, may be taken several ways. The ordinary rendering, "Leave him alone," has strong support from Exodus xxxii. 10, where the Lord says to Moses, הניחה לי, "Leave me alone," and 2 Sam. xvi. 11, and 2 Kings xxiii. 18. Or it may be a command to Judah—leave the idols to Ephraim, and have nothing to do with them. Or, again, it may be, "put them before him;" he has sought unto idols, let him have his desire; give them to him.
LXX., μέτοχος εἰδώλων, Εφραίμ, ἔθηκεν ἑαυτῷ σκάνδαλα, ἡρέτισε χαναναίους. Vulg., "Particeps idolorum Ephraim, dimitte eum." Syr., "Particeps idolorum est Aphrem, sine illum."

18  Vomited[15] is their drink,
    They have out-wantoned wantonness;
    They love (the command) "Give ye;"[16]
    Her idols[17] are (her) shame.  [lit., *shields*]

Targ., "Participes idolorum facti sunt viri domus Israel, dereliquerunt suam religionem."

18. [15] "Vomited," סר, is usually taken to mean "turned," *i.e.*, "turned off," become sour;" but why not "turned" or "returned," as we should say: they have drunken so much they can drink no more, but vomit what they have swallowed.

[16] "Give ye," הבו. It has been thought that this word, having the same termination as the preceding word, אהבו, was repeated by error of the copyist, as it is not accounted for by the LXX. and Syr., and is not found in three MSS. Others have joined the two words, and regarded them as a reduplicated form; but surely, as alliteration forms such a prominent feature throughout the verse, the difficulty must not be avoided thus. In ch. viii. 13, we have the same expression, "My give ye." In Prov. xxx. 15, it occurs again. I would take the word here as signifying, the idols are ever demanding of you more and more, and though you lose by their service, yet you love their command to make them offerings. It is worthy of remark that all false religions demand gifts of man, but true religion teaches us that God is our benefactor and gives to us.

[17] "Her idols." Literally, her shields—those whom she has chosen to be her defence, but which shall prove her disgrace.

Subjoined is the reading of the whole verse by the ancients:—LXX., Πορνεύοντες ἐξεπόρνευσαν, ἠγάπησαν ἀτιμίαν ἐξ φρυάγματος αὐτῆς. Vulg., " Separatum est convivium eorum: dilexerunt afferre ignominiam protectores ejus." Syr., "Omnes fornicati sunt, et amaverunt ignominiam et idola." Targum paraphrases, "Principes eorum multiplicaverunt convivia ex rapina, ideo erraverunt et se converterunt,

19 The spirit[18] (of wantonness) hath bound itself
בִּכְנָפֶיהָ   in her skirts;[19]
וְיֵבֹשׁוּ  And ashamed shall they be    ר
      Because of their sacrifices.

post fornicationem quam dilexerunt, ut eveniret sibi in ignominiam, proceres eorum."

19. [18] It is more agreeable to the general character of this passage to take רוח, which is generally translated "wind," in its other meaning of "spirit," and connect it with רוח in verse 12, and ch. v. 4, and translate, "the spirit of wantonness."

[19] "In her skirts." Usually rendered "wings," as belonging to the "wind"—but כנף is frequently used for the skirts or wings of a garment, (see Num. xv. 38; 1 Sam. xxiv. 6; Hag. ii. 12, &c.;) hence the rendering given above is more consistent with the context, and yields a better sense.

LXX., συστροφὴ πνεύματος σὺ εἶ ἐν ταῖς πτέρυξιν αὐτῆς. Symm., ἔδησεν ἄνεμον ἐν πτέρυξιν ἀνέμου, (perhaps αὐτοῦ.) Vulg., "Ligavit eum spiritus in alis suis." Syr., "Stridebit ventus in alis eorum."

מזבחתם. LXX., τῶν θυσιαστηρίων αὐτῶν. Vulg., "Sacrificiis suis." Syr., "Altaria sua." Targ., "Ob aras idolorum."

## CHAPTER V.

שִׁמְעוּ־זֹאת הַכֹּהֲנִים וְהַקְשִׁיבוּ בֵּית יִשְׂרָאֵל
וּבֵית הַמֶּלֶךְ הַאֲזִינוּ
כִּי לָכֶם הַמִּשְׁפָּט
כִּי־פַח הֱיִיתֶם לְמִצְפָּה
וְרֶשֶׁת פְּרוּשָׂה עַל־תָּבוֹר
וְשַׁחֲטָה שֵׂטִים הֶעְמִיקוּ

1 HEAR ye this, O priests,
   And listen, O house of Israel,
   And O house of the king, hearken ye;
   For upon you is the judgment[1] (denounced)
   Because a snare have ye been on Mizpah,[2]
   And a net spread out upon Tabor.[3]

2 And the slaughter the apostates[4] have made deep;

1. [1] "For upon you is the judgment." Many interpret these words to mean that the execution of judgment was their prerogative; others, that it was denounced against them, the Syriac, Vulgate, and Targum favour the former, the LXX. the latter interpretation.

LXX., Πρὸς ὑμᾶς ἐστι τὸ κρίμα. Vulg., "Quia vobis judicium est." Syr., "Ad vos pertinet judicium." Targum, "Nunquid vestra refert dignoscere judicium."

[2] "On Mizpah," לַמִּצְפָּה. LXX., τῇ σκοπιᾷ. Aquila, τῇ σκοπεύσει. Symm., πλατείᾳ. Vulg., "Speculationi." Targ., "Doctoribus vestris." Syr., "Speculatoribus." [Not regarding it as a proper name.]

[3] "Tabor," תָּבוֹר. LXX., ἐπὶ τὸ Ἰταβύριον. Aquila, Symm., and Theod., ἐπὶ Θαβώρ. But in the Codex Barberinus, Symm., ἐπὶ τὸ ὄριον. Theod., εἰς τὸν ἐρυμόν. Vulg., "Thabor." Targ., "Super montem excelsum." Syr., "Thabore."

2. [4] "Apostates," שֵׂטִים. Keil and Delitzsch render this word, "excesses," making it the object of the verb. Horsley, "prickers," i.e., "hunters." Fürst, in his Lexicon, "unjust judge." As שָׂטָה, the cognate verb, is used in Numb. v. 12, &c., of a woman proving unfaithful to her husband, there can be little doubt, as this figure is so frequent in our prophet, that this is the meaning here, the "apostates," i.e., forsakers of their God, have made deep, i.e., have multiplied greatly their sacrifices to their idols—the prophet does not

30          HOSEA.

וַאֲנִי   לְכֻלָּם מוּסָר

And I myself (will make deep) chastisement[5] to
   them all.
                                אֲנִי יָדַעְתִּי אֶפְרַיִם
3  I myself know Ephraim,
   And Israel is not hidden from me;  לֹא־נִכְחַד מִמֶּנִּי
   For now thou hast played the wanton, O
   Ephraim,                    כִּי עַתָּה הִזְנֵית
   Defiled is Israel.    נִטְמָא
4  They will not frame their habits   לֹא יִתְּנוּ מַעַלְלֵיהֶם
   To return to their God;   לָשׁוּב אֶל־אֱלֹהֵיהֶם
   For the spirit of wantonness is in their heart,
   But Jehovah they have not known.
5  And the Glory[6] of Israel testifies[7] to his face;

call them sacrifices, but slaughter. See, for a like example of
bitter irony, Philip. iii. 2, where St. Paul calls the observance
of circumcision,(περιτομή,) which was enforced by the Judaiz-
ing teachers after its abrogation, κατατομή.
  LXX., οἱ ἀγρεύοντες τὴνθήραν. Vulg. "Victimas." Targum, "Sacrificant idolis largissime." Syr., "Venatores
venantes, abscondentes laqueos."
  [5] The ellipsis between אֲנִי, "I," and מוּסָר, "chastisement," is generally supplied by אֶהְיֶה, "I will be," but it
seems preferable to borrow the preceding verb, as in the
text.
  5. [6] "The Glory of Israel," גְּאוֹן. It seems the most
satisfactory view that Jehovah is intended by this figure of
speech, (see Amos viii. 7,) notwithstanding the renderings
of the ancient versions, and the opinion of many commentators of note, that the idols are implied in whom Israel
then made her boast.
  Symm. and LXX., ὕβρις. Aq. and Theod., ἀλαζονεία.
Vulg., "Arrogantia." Syr., "Fastus." Targum, "Gloria."
  [7] "Testifies," עָנָה. LXX., ταπεινωθήσεται. Vulg.,
"Respondebit." Syr., "Humiliabitur." Targum, "De-
primetur."

That Israel and Ephraim
Shall fall by their iniquity,
Fallen also is Judah with them.
6 With their flocks and with their herds
Shall they go to seek Jehovah,
But shall not find Him;
He has withdrawn from them.
7 Against Jehovah have they proved false,
Because strange children they have begotten;
Now shall a month[8] consume them
With their allotments.[9]
8 Blow ye the trumpet in Gibeah,
The clarion in Ramah;
Alarm ye Beth-aven,
(Look) behind thee, O Benjamin.[10]

7. [8] "A month." This is the view taken by all the ancient versions, except the LXX. The prophet seems to say, that within a month this prediction should be fulfilled. It has been thought to refer to the reign of Shallum, who occupied the throne only one month. Delitzsch interprets it of the new moon, and its idolatrous sacrifices, which would bring down on the people calamity.

LXX., ἐρυσίβη. Aquila, νεομηνία. Symm. and Theod., μήν. Vulgate, "Mensis." Targum, "Per singulos menses." Syr. omits it altogether. Houbigant suggests, החסיל, "locust," which is purely arbitrary.

[9] "Allotments," חלקיהם, the portions, or divisions of the land allotted to each tribe. (Horsley, &c.) This is better than the comment of Pusey, Henderson, &c., that "the portions" were the idols they had chosen for themselves.

LXX., κλήρους. Vulg., "Patribus." Targ.,"Fructus terræ."

8. [10] "Behind thee." There seems some hiatus here

9  Ephraim a desolation shall be,
   In the day of punishment;
   Amongst the tribes of Israel,
   Have I made known the certainty.[11]
10 The princes of Judah have been
   Like removers of the boundary;
   Upon them will I pour out like water,
   My out-bursting-wrath.[12]
11 Overwhelmed is Ephraim,
   Crushed (is he) in judgment;
   Because he was willing,
   He went after the commandment[13] [*or foul idolatry.*]

which is best supplied by such a word as "look," or "beware of danger."

אחריך. LXX., ἐξέστη. Aq., Symm., and Theod., ὀπίσω σου. E., κατὰ νώτου σου. Vulg., "Post tergum tuum." Syr., "Clanxerunt Bethavanitæ post te Benjamin." The Targum is wholly paraphrastic in this place.

9. [11] "The certainty," נאמנה; "that which is settled and sure."
LXX., ἔδειξα πιστά. Vulg., "Ostendi fidem." Syr., "Notam faciam fidem." Targum, "Notam feci legem."

10. [12] Mark how the figure is sustained in עברתי, (from עבר,) "my outbursting wrath." They have removed the boundary, and my wrath shall overflow, as the flood, all banks and barriers.

11. [13] "The commandment," צו—found only here, and in Isa. xxviii. 10, 13—the commandment of man to go after idolatry. There seems doubt about the reading.
LXX., ὀπίσω τῶν ματαίων, "after vanities;" and so the Syriac, "Voluit sectari vanitates," as if the reading had been שוא. The Vulgate, "sordes," as if Jerome's MSS. read צוא or צואה, "filthiness." I incline to the last reading.

## CHAPTER V.

12 Therefore I myself like a moth (will be) to Ephraim,
   And as rottenness to the house of Judah.
13 Then saw Ephraim his sickness,
   And Judah his sore,
   Then went Ephraim to Asshur,
   And sent[14] to the king that loves strife;[15]
   But as for him
   He was not able to heal you,
   Neither did he remove from you the sore.
14 For I myself (will be) like a lion to Ephraim,
   And as a young lion to the house of Judah;

---

The Targum, ממון דשקר, "Mammona iniquitatis." A remarkable reading when compared with Luke xvi. 9.

13. [14] "And sent." Pocock, &c., would take Judah to be the subject of this verb, borrowed from the parallelism above.

[15] "The king that loves strife," or Jareb, ירב. This word is derived from ריב, "to contend, or strive." It seems to mean, the king who was in the habit of letting out his armies as mercenaries, to aid weaker nations, with a view to their future annexation. In this case Jareb would be Tiglath Pileser, the king of Assyria, to whom Ahaz, king of Judah, applied for assistance, (2 Kings xvi. 8, 9,) or it may refer, if Ephraim be the subject of the verb "sent," to So, king of Egypt, to whom Hoshea, the king of Israel, sent for aid, (2 Kings xvii. 4.) Some commentators make the word the name of a country or a fortress. Michaelis connects it with רב, "great," through the Syriac, and renders, "the great king."

LXX., Ἰαρείμ. Aq., δικαζόμενον. Sym., ἐκδικον. Theod., κριτήν. Vulg., "Ultorem." Syr., "Jareb." Targ., "Ut adventaret ultum eos."

I—I will tear and will go away,
I will carry off, and (there shall be) no deliverer.
15 I will go, I will return to my place
Until they suffer punishment and seek my face,
When affliction is on them they will quickly seek me.

## Chapter VI.

1 Come ye, and let us be converted to Jehovah,
Because He hath torn, and He will heal us;
He hath wounded, and He will bind us up.
2 He will quicken us, after two days;
(Even) on the third day,
He will raise us up,[1] and we shall live before his face.
3 And we shall know, we shall press on,
To know Jehovah,

2. [1] This verse has been regarded by many of the Fathers and Reformers as referring to the resurrection of our Lord; Calvin, however, and many other modern writers expound it as a prediction of the resuscitation of the nation. Horsley takes a middle course, and considers the passage as adaptively prophetic of the resurrection of our Lord. Critics, when dealing with particular points, often seem forgetful of general principles. One leading ground-thought of the Old Testament seems to be the identification of Israel's king with Israel's kingdom, and vice versâ, (see, e.g., ch. xi. 1;) hence what is here predicated of the nation is intended to be a propheticotypical statement about Messiah. There can be no doubt that this is the true reference. The Lord arose on the third day, and in Him His people rose. It is remarkable that the words συνεζωοποίησε and συνήγειρε, exact equivalents of the two verbs in this verse, are used by St. Paul in Eph. ii. 5, 6, and with seeming reference to this passage.

יחיינו. LXX., ὑγιάσει ἡμᾶς. Aq. and Symm., ἀναζωώσει ἡμᾶς. E., ὑγιεῖς ἀποδείξει ἡμᾶς. Syr., "Vivos servabit nos." Vulg., "Vivificabit nos." The paraphrase of the Targum is worthy of notice, as bearing on the doctrine of the text: "Vita donabit nos in diebus consolationis qui venturi sunt, in die resurrectionis mortuorum suscitabit nos, et vivemus coram eo."

Like the morning, fixed[2] is His coming forth;[3]
And He shall come like the rain upon us,
Like the latter rain watering the earth.
4 What shall I do to thee, O Ephraim?
What shall I do to thee, O Judah?
וְחַסְדְּכֶם For your piety[4] is like the morning cloud,
And like the dew early departing.
5 Therefore, I have hewed (them) by the prophets;
I have slain them with the words of my mouth:
And the decrees concerning thee[5] (as) light shall go forth.

3. [2] "Fixed." The time of Messiah's appearance was predetermined in the counsels of the Father, and revealed in the prophetic almanack of Daniel, (ch. ix. 25, 26,) that Israel might know the date of the coming dawn. The period of Christ's first advent was made known, because acceptance of Him as a sacrifice and atonement was necessary to salvation; the hour of His second advent is not disclosed, because not necessary to salvation.

[3] "His coming forth." The Incarnation is here alluded to. (Comp. John xvi. 28, "I came forth from the Father," ἐξῆλθον. LXX., ὡς ὄρθρον ἕτοιμον εὑρήσομεν αὐτόν. Symm., ὡς ὄρθρος βεβαία ἡ ἐπιφάνεια αὐτοῦ. Vulg., "Quasi diluculum preparatus est egressus ejus." Syr., "Ut ad auroram cujus certus est exortus." Targ., "Quasi lux matutina."

4. [4] "Your piety," חסדכם. חסד, when referred to God, signifies "grace," "favour," "good will;" when to men, "grace" received, and the fruits of grace, "piety," "religion,"—here their profession of these spiritual qualities. LXX., τὸ δὲ ἔλεος ὑμῶν. E., ὁ γὰρ περὶ ὑμᾶς οἰκτιρμός. Vulg., "Misericordia vestra." Syr., "Bonitas vestra." Targ., "Benignitas vestra."

5. [5] "The decrees concerning thee," מִשְׁפָּטֶיךָ—literally, "thy judgments;" objective, "the things adjudged or

## CHAPTER VI.

זֶבַח וְלֹא חָפַצְתִּי הֶסֶד כִּי
6 For piety⁶ I desired and not sacrifice;
וְדַעַת And the knowledge of God אֱלֹהִים
מֵעֹלוֹת Above burnt offerings.
וְהֵמָּה 7 But as for them,
Like Adam⁷ have they transgressed a covenant,
It was there they proved false to me.

decreed for thee." Here evidently, from the context, in a good sense, as the stern rebukes of the prophets were for their good. This is a not unfrequent form of speech—see Rom. xi. 31, τῷ ὑμετέρῳ ἐλέει, "your mercy," *i.e.*, the mercy showed to you; 1 Cor. xv. 31, νὴ τὴν ὑμετέραν καύχησιν, "by your rejoicing," *i.e.*, by the rejoicing I have on your account. The LXX., Syr., and Targ. read, מִשְׁפָּטִי, "my judgment," which was probably an explanatory gloss.

LXX., τὸ κρίμα μου. The other versions, ἡ δικαιοκρισία. Vulg., "Judicia tua." Syr. and Targ., "Judicium meum."

6. ⁶ "Piety." This passage derives interest and importance from its being twice quoted by our Lord, (Matt. ix. 9, and xii. 7.) חֶסֶד is equivalent to grace and piety, (see previous note.) True heart-religion is better than a thousand sacrifices. Pusey refers the "mercy" to the duties enforced in the second table of the law, and "sacrifice" to those of the first; he compares this text with 1 John iv. 20. Sacrifice without performance of our duties to our fellow-creatures is useless. If any reference is made to the two tables of the law, the knowledge of God would seem rather to point to the first table.

7. ⁷ "Like Adam," כְּאָדָם. Clearly a proper name, not "men" generally. This latter interpretation much weakens the charge of unfaithfulness. God made a covenant with Adam, he broke it. God made a covenant with Israel, they broke that also. (Compare Job. xxxi. 33, Ps. xlix. 12, and Ps. lxxxii. 7.)

LXX., ὡς ἄνθρωπος. Syr., "Ut filius hominis." Vulg., "Sicut Adam." Targum, "Sicuti generationes priscæ." Michaelis proposed the reading, כֶּאֱדֹם, "like Edom."

8   As for Gilead,[8]
    It is a city of idol makers,[9]
    Tracked-with-heel-marks of blood.[10]
9   And as gangs lie in wait for a man,
    (So) a company of priests
    Commit murder along the road to Shechem ;[11]
    For purposed-crime they have committed.

8. [8] "Gilead," *i.e.*, Ramoth Gilead, a city of refuge; hence the reference in the " tracked-with-heel-marks of blood." In 2 Kings xv. 25, we are told that when Pekah killed Pekahiah, there were with him fifty men of the Gileadites, who aided him in the evil deed; probably there is a reference here to that occurrence.

[9] " Of idol makers." This rendering is to be preferred to the more vague translation of the authorised version, " of them that work iniquity." LXX., ἐργαζομένη μάταια, an expression that indicated "idols." Vulg., " Civitas operantium idolum." Syr., " Urbs illa operantium iniquitatem." Targum, " Vim inferentium."

[10] " Tracked-with-heel-marks of blood," עקבה מדם. LXX., ταράσσουσα ὕδωρ. Aq., περικαμπὴς ἀπὸ αἵματος. Symm., διώκται ἀπὸ αἵματος. E., ὑποσκελίζουσα καὶ δολοφονοῦσα. Vulg., " Supplantata sanguine." Syr., " Sanguine conspersa." Targum, " Effundentium sanguinem innocentium."

9. [11] " To Shechem," שכמה. Authorised version, "by consent;" margin, "with one shoulder," or " to Shechem." The last rendering is the best. The ancient versions regard the word as a proper name. This was also a city of refuge, and therefore of the priests and Levites. The charge against them is a solemn one, that these cities, which were intended to be refuges to preserve life, had been made by them snares and dens of death.

LXX., Σίκιμα. Aquila, " Humeros." Symm., "Sichem." Theod., " In dorso." Syr., "Sechim." Vulg., " de Sichem." Targum, כהף חד , " Consensu uno."

10  In the house of Israel,
    I have seen an awful sight;
    There wantonness (is found) in Ephraim,
    Defiled is Israel.
11  Also, O Judah,
    He hath appointed a harvest [12] for thee,
    When I turn again the captivity of my people.

11. [12] "A harvest." What is the meaning of this? Horsley interprets in a good sense, as a figure of the ingathering of the faithful. Secker and Newcome, in a bad sense, "The time of being cut off, as ripe for destruction." Henderson, the punishment, in all probability, which is recorded in 2 Chron. xxviii. 6, 8. Pusey, the restoration after the Babylonish captivity, when the kingdom of Israel suffered final destruction, but rich mercies were in store for Judah. This interpretation would furnish an example of the quick transitions for which our prophet is so remarkable—a sudden gleam of mercy darting out from behind the storm-clouds of judgment. On the other hand, the whole context, and the character of the passage itself, combined with the fact that all the ancient versions seem to favour the idea of judgment rather than of mercy, incline us to the view that as punishments have fallen upon Israel, Judah may also prepare herself for a like visitation. If we take the verb in a future perfect sense, the verse may be expounded, "when or after I shall have turned the captivity of my people," by bringing them back from Babylon, Judah by their rejection of Messiah will bring down upon themselves the heaviest judgments, and will fall before their enemies as corn before the reaper.

LXX., καὶ Ἰούδα, ἄρχου τρυγᾶν σεαυτῷ. Symm., καὶ σοὶ Ἰούδα ἀπόκειται θερισμός. E., ἀλλὰ καὶ σὺ Ἰούδα παρεσκεύαζες αὐτὸν εἰς τὸ ἐκθερισθῆναι. Vulg., "Pone messem tibi." Syr., "Para tibi vindemiam." Targum, "Ad eos pariter pertinget reatus."

## Chapter VII.

1 When I healed Israel
   Then was revealed the iniquity of Ephraim,
וְרָעוֹת    And the wickedness of Samaria;
   Because they have made an idol;
   Therefore a thief shall come (in),[1]
   A gang shall plunder in the street.
2 And they say not in their heart;[2]
כָּל־רָעָתָם    All their wickedness I remember;
   Now their actions have beset them,
   Before my face are they.
בְּרָעָתָם 3   With their wickedness they make glad the king; מֶלֶךְ
   And with lies the princes.
4 All of them are adulterers,
   Like an oven heated by the baker,
   He leaves off stirring (it),
   From (the time of) kneading the dough till it is leavened.[3]

1. [1] "Shall come in," יָבוֹא. LXX., εἰσελεύσεται. Symm., εἰσῆλθεν. E., ἐστιν ἔνδον. Vulg., "Ingressus est." Syr., "Ingrediebatur." Targum, "In domibus."

2. [2] לְלִבָּבָם, literally, "*to* their heart." בְּ, "in," is found in several MSS., and is supported by Syr., Vulg., and Targum.

4. [3] The meaning of the comparison in this passage seems to be that the nation, as represented by its leading men, had some plan or plot in their minds, to seduce the king on some favourable occasion, such as his coronation day or his birth-day, (see Matt. xiv. 6, 7,) to consent to some act of wickedness—most likely to seek aid of some heathen power, Egypt or Assyria, (v. 11.) Hence they are compared (1) to adulterers, and (2) because the intensity of their desire to carry out this measure was so great, to an oven heated so fiercely that it stood

5   In the day of our king,[4]
מלכנו יום

in no need of fuel, though left all night unfed. The baker would seem to refer to some leader of the movement, who wished to remain in the background. The fifth verse explains and applies the figure of the oven—they heated the king with wine, till he gave in to the demands of the ungodly faction. In the sixth verse the sleeping of the baker or ringleader is explanatory of the ceasing of the same person to stir the oven-furnace all night, (v. 4.) In the seventh verse the result of the manœuvre is given us in the destruction of the rulers and princes themselves, and in the eighth verse the punishment of the people, who are compared to a cake in the oven which has not been turned, and is therefore burned and utterly destroyed.

LXX., Πάντες μοιχεύοντες ὡς κλίβανος καιόμενος εἰς πέψιν κατακαύματος ἀπὸ τῆς φλογός, ἀπὸ φυράσεως στέατος, ἕως τοῦ ζυμωθῆναι αὐτό.   E., Ἅπαντες εἰς τὸ μοιχεύειν ἐκπυρούμενοι, ὡς ὀπτάνιον ὑπὸ τοῦ πέσσοντος. Ἐπαύσατο πρὸς ὀλίγον ἡ πόλις τοῦ φυράματος κοινωνίας, καὶ μετὰ μικρὸν πᾶσα ἐζυμώθη.  Syr., " Omnes principes eorum mœchantur, ut clibanus ardens ad coctionem panis; deficiet ab urbe subigens massam donec firmentetur."   Vulg., " Quasi clibanus succensus a coquente; quievit paululum civitas a commistione fermenti, donec firmentaretur totum." Targ., " Œstuant instar clibani quem accendit sibi pistor quamobrem migrabunt ex civitatibus suis ab eo tempore quo subacta fuit massa antequam firmentaretur."

It will thus be seen that Syr., Vulg., and Targ. take עיר as " city," with the preposition מ, " from the city."   Horsley מעיר, a substantive from Hiphil of עור, " excitator," (a stoker,) a man whose business it is to stir up the fire of the oven.

5. [4] " Day of our king," either the day of his accession, or his birthday. There is high authority for the plural number here, " our kings," (see next page.) The king was most probably Hoshea.

42                                HOSEA.

  The princes made (him) ill[5] with heat from
      (drinking) wine;
  He stretched out his hand with blasphemers.
6 When they brought near their oven-like heart in
      their plot;[6]
  All the night long their baker had slept,
  (Yet) in the morning
  It was burning like a fire of flame.
7 They are all hot as an oven,
  And they devour their judges;
  All their kings have fallen,[7]
  There is none among them that calleth on me.
8 As for Ephraim,
  With the nations he hath prostituted himself;

  Twenty-two MSS. and Syr. read מלכינו. LXX. also, ἡμέραι τῶν βασιλέων. Theod., ἡμέρα βασιλέως. Vulg., "Regis." Syr., "Regum." Targ., "Regem."
  [5] "Made him ill," החלו. Some derive this word from חלל, to "begin," and take חמת as an infinitive mood, and render, "began to make him hot with wine." Others read חֵמֶת, "bottle,"—"made him sick with a bottle of wine." The most simple and satisfactory interpretation is that of making the king ill with *fever* brought on by wine-bibbing; especially as in the seventh verse we have the cognate verb, יחמו, "they are hot."
  LXX., ἤρξαντο οἱ ἄρχοντες θυμοῦσθαι ἐξ οἴνου. Syr., "Cœperunt magnates vino furere." Vulg., "Cœperunt principes furere a vino." Targ., "Exorsi sunt magnates compotare cum eo vinum."
  6. [6] "In their plot," בארבם. LXX., ἐν τῷ καταράσσειν αὐτούς. Aq., Symm., and Theod., ἐνεδρεύειν. Syr. and Targ., "In insidiis suis." Vulg., "Cum insidiaretur eis."
  7. [7] The murders of Zachariah, Shallum, Pekahiah, and Pekah are here referred to. (See 2 Kings, xv.)

## CHAPTER VII.

Ephraim has become a cake that has not been turned.

9 Strangers have devoured his strength,
Yet he hath not known (it),
Also hoar hair is sprinkled on him,
Yet he hath not known (it).

10 And the Glory[8] of Israel testifies to his face;
Yet they return not to Jehovah their God,
And they seek Him not for all this.

11 And Ephraim became
Like a silly dove, without understanding;
Egypt they call on, Asshur they go to.[9]

12 As they are going
I will spread on them my net,
Like a bird of the air I will bring them down;
I will punish them
According to the announcement[10] made to their assembly.

10. [8] "Glory," see ch. v. 5.

11. [9] The history connected with this verse is found in 2 Kings xvii. 1—6, where we read that Hoshea, the king of Israel, made an alliance with So, king of Egypt, and thus was guilty of conspiracy against Shalmaneser, king of Assyria, who, in consequence of this defection, came up and took Samaria, and led Israel away captive; thus, though they called upon Egypt for assistance, yet they went to Assyria.

12. [10] "According to the announcement," כשמע. What they have heard from me—my message to them.

LXX., ἐν τῇ ἀκοῇ τῆς θλίψεως αὐτῶν. Aquila, κατὰ ἀκοῆς τῆς συναγωγῆς. Symm., κατ᾽ ἀκοῆς τῆς μαρτυρίας. Syr., "Secundum auditum contestationis eorum." Vulg., "Secundum auditionem cœtus eorum." Targ., "Propterea quod sunt obsecuti suis consiliis."

13  Woe to them because they have strayed from me,
    Destruction unto them[11] because they have trespassed against me;
    Yet I myself redeemed them,
    But as for them,
    They have spoken against me lies.
14  And they have not cried to me with their heart,
    Though they howl on their beds ;[12]
    For corn and must they gather together,[13]
    They rebel against me.
15  And I exercised,[14]
    (And) I strengthened their arms ;
    Yet against me they meditate evil.
16  They shall return to a no-God,[15]

13. [11] "Destruction unto them," שׁד להם. LXX., δείλαιοί εἰσιν. Aq., προνομὴ αὐτοῖς. Symm., διαφθορά. Theod., "Miseria." E., ἐκπορθήσονται. Syr., "Væ illis." Vulg. and Targ., "Væ eis."

14. [12] "Howl on their beds"—in a morbid and discontented spirit, as Ahab. (1 Kings xxi. 4.)

[13] "They gather together," i.e., in their idol-temples, to ask of their gods for the necessaries of life. Instead of יתגוררו, "they gather together," some MSS., which are followed by LXX., read, יתגודדו, κατετέμνοντο, "they cut themselves," that is, in the worship of Baal, as was the case when Elijah contended with the priests of Baal.

LXX., κατετέμνοντο, ἐπαιδεύθησαν ἐν ἐμοί. E., ἀπέστησάν μου. The other versions, ἐξέκλιναν ἀπ' ἐμοῦ. Syr., "Gemuerunt." Vulg., "Super triticum et vinum ruminabant." Targ., "Ululant."

15. [14] Some render this hemistich, "I chastened — I strengthened," i.e., I tried both experiments—punishing and blessing—to no purpose.

16. [15] "To a no-god." לא על. Some regard על as ab-

## CHAPTER VII.

They have become like a deceitful bow,
Their princes shall fall by the sword for the provocation of their tongue;
This (shall be) their ridicule in the land of Egypt.

breviated from עליון, "the Most High," though such contraction is not found elsewhere. One MS. reads, אל, "God." Others take על as an adverb, "sursum," "on high." Others, again, as a substantive, following the Vulgate, על, "a yoke,"—the yoke of the Mosaic law. The interpretation which refers, על, either to God or His dwelling-place, which practically teaches the same lesson, is on the whole to be preferred.

LXX., εἰς οὐδέν. Symm., εἰς τὸ μὴ ἔχειν ζυγόν. E., ἄνευ ζυγοῦ. Syr., "Obliquarunt se nulla de causa." Vulg., "Absque jugo." Targ., "Aversi sunt ut deficerent a lege, non quòd malum intulerim eis."

## Chapter VIII.

1 To thy mouth a trumpet!
 An eagle,[1] against the house of Jehovah!
 Because they have transgressed my covenant,
 And against my law have they trespassed.
2 To me shall they cry;
 "O My God," we know thee,—
 (We are) Israel.[2]
3 Israel hath rejected

1. [1] "An eagle." The כ in כנשר, is not the כ of comparison, but rather of assertion.

LXX. renders εἰς κόλπον αὐτῶν ὡς γῆ; the sense of which is not very clear. Aq., Symm., Theod., "In gutture tuo sit tuba." Vulg., "In gutture tuo sit tuba quasi aquila." Syr., "Os tuum ut buccina sit." Targum, "Propheta gutture tuo clamita quasi in tuba."

2. [2] "Israel." Some insert, as Houbigant, אלהי, "God of," before Israel. If the word is referred to God, Ps. xxiv. 7, "O Jacob," would furnish a parallel. Many ancient versions omitted it altogether, (see below.) The English version regards it as a noun of multitude, the nominative case to the verb "cry," "Israel shall cry." But the position of the words is against this translation. Delitzsch takes the word in apposition to the nominative of the verb "we know thee"—we, Israel. The true bearing of the passage seems to be the same as in Matt. vii. 22, &c., "Lord, have we not prophesied in Thy name," &c. The people presume upon their pedigree from the saints of old, and hence cry in their calamity, "O God we know Thee; we are Israel." This interpretation is supported by the Targum. (See below.)

One MS., and originally another, omit the word ישראל, and so also the LXX. and Syr. It is found in the Vulgate. Targum, "Quandoquidem sumus populus tuus Israel."

## CHAPTER VIII.     47

The Gracious One ;³
An enemy shall pursue him.⁴

4 They themselves made kings,⁵ but not with my consent,
They made princes, but I recognized them not;
With their silver and their gold,
They have made themselves idols,
To the end that (Israel) should be cut off.

5 (My wrath) has rejected⁶ thy calf, O Samaria,
My wrath is hot against them;

3. ³ "The Gracious One," (see ch. iii. 5, and xiv. 2.) Some eminent Jewish commentators, and Œcolampadius, interpret טוב, in this place of God. The word seems throughout Hosea to be a synonym of Messiah. The idea contained in the former verse, is continued in this; they professed to be the people of God; they called Him, Lord, Lord, but did not do His will. They were forerunners of the generation that boasted, "we have Abraham to our father," but would not come to Abraham's "seed," that they might have life.

⁴ "Shall pursue him," יִרְדְּפוֹ. Many MSS., Syr., Targ., read יִרְדְּפוּ, "Shall pursue them."

4. ⁵ "They themselves made kings." The ten-tribe kingdom was but a faction against the true Hebrew monarchy of David's line.

5. ⁶ "Hath rejected," &c., זנח עגלך. Here is evidently a reference to the third verse; Israel has rejected the "Gracious One," so God hath rejected her idolatry. The difficulty here lies in the subject to זנח. Fürst, in Lex. s. v., takes "God" to be the nominative understood. The English version, Horsley, and Pusey, "Thy calf hath cast thee off; as thou hast rejected God, so thy idol rejects thee." Aquila and Theod. make it imperative, and are followed by Newcome, "Remove far from thee." The

How long, will they not embrace pure religion ?⁷
6 Because it even (came) from Israel,
A smith made it,
Therefore is it no God,
So (into) powder ⁸ shall be turned,
The calf of Samaria.

Vulg. takes it passively. Henderson translates, " Thy calf is abominable." The antithesis, however, does not seem to be between their rejecting of God and their calf rejecting them, but rather between their rejecting of God and God rejecting their idol. It would therefore be preferable to supply the noun from the next clause, " My wrath," אפי.
LXX., ἀπότριψαι τὸν μόσχον σου. Symm., ἀπεβλήθη ὁ μόσχος σου. Aquila, ἀπώθησον τὸν μόσχον σου. Theod., ἀπόρριψαι. E., ἀπόβλητός σου ἐστιν ὁ μόσχος. Syr., " Erraverunt ob vitulum tuum." Vulg., " Projectus est vitulus tuus." Targ., " Erraverunt ad vitulum."
⁷ " Pure religion," נקין. LXX., καθαρισθῆναι. Aq., ἀθωωθῆναι. Symm., καθαρθῆναι. Vulg., " Emendari." Syr., " Innocenter agere." Targum, " Se purgare."
6. Two points are insisted upon here—(1) that the calf was only the work of man, (2) that Israel was the guilty nation that made it.
⁸ " Powder," שבבים. There has been much discussion whether this word, which only occurs here, should be rendered " flames " or " pieces." The reference is clearly as Hengstenberg has pointed out in his " Veracity of the Pentateuch," vol. i., p. 119, to the destruction of Aaron's calf in the wilderness, though the learned professor's argument would as strongly support the translation of " little pieces " or " powder," as " fire," for which he so strongly contends.
LXX. and Theod., πλανῶν. Symm., ἀκαταστατῶν. E , ῥεμβεύων. Syr., " Ad errorem fuit." Vulg., " Aranearum telas." Targ., " In minuta tabularum redigetur."

7   Because the wind they sow,
     Therefore the hurricane they shall reap;
     Not a stalk shall he have,
     The blossom shall not yield corn,
     If perchance it should yield
     Strangers shall swallow it up.
8   Swallowed up is Israel,
     Now have they become among the nations
     Like a vessel in which is no delight.
9   For they went up to Asshur,
     (Like) a wild-ass straying alone by himself;
     As for Ephraim they have paid fee for loves.[9]
10  Also because they have paid the love-fee [10] among
         the nations,
     Now will I gather them;[11]
     And they shall be in woe speedily[12]

9. [9] Probably this refers to Menahem's payment of a thousand talents of silver to Pul, (2 Kings xv. 19.)

10. [10] "Paid the love-fee." It will be seen below that another reading will give the sense, "They are given over among the nations." A very suitable sense, but it is more likely that the prophet would repeat the word just used in the preceding verse.

יִתְנוּ. Two MSS. read יֻתְּנוּ, "they are given over." LXX., παραδοθήσονται. But E. reads as the Hebrew text, ἀλλὰ καὶ ὅταν μισθώσηται ἔθνη. Vulg., "Cum mercede conduxerint nationes." Syr., "Tradantur."

[11] "Gather them." That is, the nations to whom they have sought, but who shall prove their oppressors.

[12] "And they shall be in woe speedily." These words have given rise to much difference of opinion, the ancient versions (see next page) derive ויחלו, from חול, "to desist from, to rest," &c. Horsley, Newcome, &c., derive it from

On account of the burden (laid on their) king (and) princes.[13]

חול, in the sense of "to be in pain or sorrow." Delitzsch in the sense of "to begin"—"they will begin to diminish." It seems preferable to refer it to this verb in its frequent application to the pains of labour, and compare it with Matt. xxiv. 8, πάντα δὲ ταῦτα ἀρχὴ ὠδίνων, "But all these things are the beginning of sorrows," literally, of "birth pangs." All Israel's visitations on account of sin were but types of this last great tribulation of which our Lord here speaks. For וַיָּחֵלּוּ, ten MSS. read וַיָּחֵלוּ.

[13] "King (and) princes." This is regarded by some as a case of asyndeton—the copula being omitted. This is supplied by some MSS., and by all the ancient versions, and many learned critics. Others, as English version, translate "the king of princes," and quote Isa. x. 8, "Are not my princes altogether kings," in support of this theory. But in chap. vii. 5, and xiii. 10, we have express mention made of Israel's king and princes, and their evil doings. The former passage, so contiguous to this in position, and referring to the punishment of Israel, must surely therefore point to Israel's king and princes. The "burden" will therefore be subjective and not objective, as in Isa. xiii. 1, xv. 1, xvii. 1, 4, &c. And the meaning will be "they shall suffer woe on account of the burden laid on their king and princes." (See 2 Kings xv. 19, &c.)

The renderings of the whole passage in the ancient versions, read thus:—LXX., καὶ κοπάσουσι μικρὸν τοῦ χρίειν βασιλέα καὶ ἄρχοντας. Aquila, καὶ λιτανεύσωσιν ὀλίγον ἀπὸ ἅρματος βασιλέως καὶ ἀρχόντων. Symm., καὶ μενοῦσιν βράχει ἀπὸ φόβου βασιλέων καὶ διαλείψουσι τοῦ χρίειν. Theod., καὶ διαλείψουσι τοῦ χρίειν. Syr., "Ut quiescant paulisper ab onere regum et principum." Vulg., "Ab onere regis et principum." Targ., "Si paulisper sapiant, auferam ab eis dominium regum et principum." It will be seen by the above that the versions

## CHAPTER VIII. 51

11  Because Ephraim has multiplied altars to commit sin ;
    They have become to him altars to commit sin.[14]
12  I write [15] to him,
    The weighty things [16] of my law ;
    As a strange thing are they accounted.

supplied the copula between מלך שרים, which is also the reading of twenty MSS., and originally of ten others.

11. [14] For the second לחטא, "to commit sin," the LXX. has ἠγαπημένα. Vulg., "In delictum." Syr., "Ad crimen ingens." Targ., "In ruinam."

12. [15] "I write," or "will write." The future form is employed to mark the abiding validity of the law, which though written centuries ago, comes with fresh force to each succeeding generation.

[16] "The weighty things." (See the readings of the ancient versions below.) Delitzsch remarks, "These words refer unquestionably to the great number of laws written in the Mosaic *Thorah*, רבו, according to the *Chethib* רִבּוֹ, with ה dropped, equivalent to רבבה, as in 1 Chron. xxix. 7, ten thousand, myriads. The Masoretes, who supposed the number to be used in an arithmetical sense, altered it as conjecturally unsuitable, into רִבֵּי, 'multitudes,' although רֹב does not occur anywhere else in the plural. The expression 'the myriads of my law' is hyperbolical, to indicate the almost innumerable multitude of the different commandments contained in the law." Horsley takes רבי in the sense of "*masters*." "The masters of my law are accounted as it were an alien race." The ordinary rendering, however, of "great" or "weighty," has most to recommend it, as it is possible the Lord Jesus quoted the passage in Matt. xxiii. 23, τὰ βαρύτερα τοῦ νόμου. "The weightier matters of the law."

רבו, K'ri רִבֵּי, plural of רֹב. LXX., καταγράφω αὐτῷ πλῆθος

13  As to the sacrifices of my (command) "give,"
    "give,"[17]
    They shall sacrifice flesh and eat it,
    Jehovah will not accept them;
    Now shall He remember their iniquity, and visit
        their sins,
    They themselves to Egypt shall return.
14  And Israel hath forgotten His Maker
    And built temples,
    And as for Judah,
    He hath multiplied fortified cities;[18]

καὶ τὰ νόμιμα αὐτοῦ εἰς ἀλλότρια ἐλογίσθησαν. Aquila, πληθυμένους νόμους. Symm., πλῆθος νόμων μου. Vulg., "Multiplices leges meas." Syr., "Multitudinem legum mearum." Targum, "Multiplicitatem legis meæ."

13. [17] "My (command) give, give." Fürst, following Kimchi, derives this word הבהבי, "my burnt-offerings," from הוב, "to roast;" but surely when we look back to chap. iv. 18, and find the form הבו applied to the exaction of the idols—"give, give,"—we naturally infer that the word is here employed to express the Lord's command to bring Him their sacrifices, but as the law was accounted as a strange thing by them, their offerings therefore could not be accepted.

זבחי הבהבי. LXX., Θυσιαστήρια τὰ ἠγαπημένα. Aquila, Οὐσίας φέρε φέρε Οὐσιάζουσιν. Symm., Θυσίας ἐπαλλήλους Οὐσιάζουσι. Theod., Οὐσίας μεταφορῶν ἐθυσίασαν. Vulg., "Hostias offerent." Syr., "Victimas selectas sacrificant." Targ., "Sacrificant quæ ex rapina colligunt."

14. [18] See 2 Chron. xxvi. 9, 10, where we read that Uzziah of Judah, the contemporary of Menahem of Israel, built towers in Jerusalem and the desert.

Therefore I will cast fire on his cities,[19]
And it shall devour their palaces.[20]

[19] See for fulfilment of this prophecy, 2 Kings xviii. 13.

[20] The suffixes in בעריו, literally, "his cities," and ארמנתיה, "her palaces," are of different genders; the masculine referring to the people, and the feminine to the land; or the feminine suffix may refer to each of the cities, as though it were, " the fire shall consume his cities, and the palaces in each of them."

## Chapter IX.

1 Rejoice not, O Israel, to exultation as¹ the peoples,
  For thou hast played the wanton away from thy God;
  Thou hast loved a love-fee,
  Upon all corn threshing-floors.
2 The threshing-floor and wine-press shall not feed them;
  And the must shall fail her.²
3 They shall not dwell in the land of Jehovah;
  But Ephraim shall return to Egypt,
  And in Asshur unclean food shall they eat.
4 They shall not pour out to Jehovah wine,
  Neither shall they mingle³ it to Him;
  As for their sacrifices,
  (They shall be) as the bread of mourning⁴ to them,
  All that eat it shall be defiled;

1. ¹ Thirteen MSS., originally five more, read ב "among" instead of כ "as."

2. ² More than 20 MSS., and all the ancient versions and Targum, read בם, "them."

4. ³ "Mingle," יערבו. It is preferable to take this word in this its primary sense, referring to the "wine" as its object, rather than to make "sacrifices" in the next line the subject, and to take this verb in the sense of "please."

LXX., οὐκ ἥδυναν. Syr., "Neque condient sacrificia." Vulg., "Non placebunt." Targ., "Nec suscipientur cum beneplacito sacrificia."

⁴ "Bread of mourning," לחם אונים. As the food of those who eat in a house where a corpse is lying. All that came in contact with a dead body were unclean, (see Numb. xix. 14.)

LXX., ὡς ἄρτος πένθους. Syr., "Panis angustiæ." Vulg., "Panis lugentium." Targ., "Panis abominabilis."

> Because their bread for their souls
> Shall not come into the house of Jehovah.
> 5 What will ye do on the day of festival;
> And on the day of the feast of Jehovah?
> 6 Lo, though they go away from destruction,
> (Yet) Egypt shall gather them,
> Memphis[5] shall bury them;
> As for their silver valuables,[6]
> The nettle shall possess them,
> The thorn (shall be) in their tents.
> 7 Come are the days of the visitation,
> Come are the days of the retribution;
> (Then) shall Israel know,
> That foolish was the (false) prophet,
> That guilty of folly[7] was the man (who pretended to) inspiration

6. [5] "Memphis," מֹף. Aquila, ἐκ στόματος. LXX., Syr., Vulg., and Targum, "Memphis."

[6] "Valuables," מחמד. The LXX. took this word as a proper name, Μαχμάς. Aquila and Symm., τὰ ἐπιθυμήματα. Syr., "Exquisitum." Vulg. and Targ., "Desiderabile." Three MSS. read לנפשם for לכספם, "the desire of their souls," instead of "the valuables of their silver."

7. [7] "Guilty of folly," משגע. LXX., ὁ παρεξεστηκώς. Aquila, ἐπίληπτος. Symm., ἐνεός. Syr., "Stultum." Vulg., "Insanum."

The prophet in this verse is carried on to the day, then close at hand, when the vengeance predicted should be inflicted on the apostate nation; in that day Israel shall know by bitter experience that the false prophet, who pretended to a knowledge of the future, and preached "peace, peace," when there was no peace, was only an impostor and a madman.

Because of the greatness of their iniquity,
And the great provocation.

8 A watchman[8] (was) Ephraim with my God;
(Now) the (false) prophet is a fowler's snare in all his ways,
Provocation in the house of his god.

9 They have deeply corrupted (themselves,) as in the days of Gibeah;

8. [8] "A watchman," &c. A series of contrasts between what Ephraim was formerly, and what Ephraim became afterwards, commences here. These contrasts form texts, as it were, for the remarks which follow each, (see verses 10 and 13; ch. x. 1, xi. 1, xiii. 1.) In this place Ephraim is reminded of the high and holy position he held with God in the former days of his faithfulness, when he kept his eye on the law, and watched for revelations from God; and with this is compared his present apostacy in listening to the false prophets who led the people astray into idolatry, which brought down judgments upon them. Mark the contrast between "my God," the God of the prophet Hosea, the true God, and "his god," the idol-god that Ephraim had set up and served. A few MSS. read אלהיו, "his god," but it is merely an emendation to escape a supposed difficulty.

The interpretations of this passage are very various. The English version renders "the watchman of Ephraim," but צפה is not in the construct case. Some, "Ephraim is a spy with (*i.e.*, against) my God." Others, "Ephraim is on the look-out for revelations besides those that come from my God." Others, "Ephraim is looking out for help from my God." Others again, "Ephraim seeks revelations still from the God of Hosea, because he distrusts the false prophets."

LXX., Σκοπὸς 'Εφραὶμ μετὰ Θεοῦ. Syr. and Vulg., "Speculator cum deo meo." Targ., "Prospicientes qui sunt ex domo Israel quo permaneat eis cultus idolorum suorum."

He will remember their iniquity,
He will visit their sins.

10 As grapes in the desert,
I found Israel,
As the firstling on the fig-tree in its beginning,
I saw your fathers;
But they themselves went after Baal-peor,
And separated themselves to (that) shame,
And became as abominable as their (idol) love.

11 As for Ephraim,
Like a bird shall their glory fly away;
(So that there shall be) no birth, and no bearing,
and no conception.

12 But if they rear up their sons,
I will destroy them that there shall not be a man;
Thus woe also (shall be) to them when I depart
from them.⁹

12. ⁹ " When I depart from them." The readings of the ancient versions of this passage are given below. That of the LXX., followed by Theodotion, is remarkable : " My flesh is of them." Lyra charged this as one of the passages which the Jews had altered. Raimundus, in his " Pugio Fidei," says that whereas it should be read בשרי, " my flesh," or בשורי, " my incarnation," the Jews made it the same as if spelt with ס instead of שׁ, and derive it from סור, " to turn away." Ribera refuted this notion on the score that the Hebrew was uncorrupted in the times of the Vulgate and the Targum, which are like the Hebrew text as it now stands, and also, that if it favoured anything, it would prove that Messiah would come of the ten tribes, and so support the Jewish theory of Messiah Ben Joseph, (see Pocock, *in loco*.)

בשורי מהם. Three MSS. have ס instead of שׁ. LXX., σάρξ μου ἐξ αὐτῶν. Aq., ἐκκλίναντός μου ἀπ' αὐτῶν. Theod.,

58                               HOSEA.

13  Ephraim was planted in (his) place,
    Like as I have seen a rock;[10]
    But Ephraim
    Would lead out to the murderer his sons.
14  Therefore give them, O Jehovah,
    What shouldest thou give?
    Give them a womb that miscarries,
    And breasts that are dry.
15  All their wickedness (was) in Gilgal,
    For (it was) there (that) I hated them,
    Because of the wickedness of their actions,
    From my house I will banish them;

"Caro mea ex eis." Vulg., "Cum recessero ab eis." Syr.,
"Ultionem sumpturus sum ab eis." Targ., "Cum sustulero
majestatem meam ab eis."

13. [10] "Like as I have seen a rock," כאשר ראיתי לצור.
This passage has created much difficulty, both with ancient
and modern interpreters, (see versions below.) Some take
צור as a proper name, "Tyre," and others in the primary
sense of "Rock." The latter seems to yield by far the most
consistent meaning—whilst Ephraim was obedient to God's
commandments, he was fixed like a rock in a lovely spot, and
that spot the goodly inheritance that God had given him, but
he would bring up his children to idolatry, and so lead them
out to the murderer. What therefore will be the most fitting
punishment for such an one?—the denying him the gift of
any more children, and the cutting off of those he already
possesses.

לצור וג׳. LXX., εἰς Θήραν παρέστησαν τὰ τέκνα αὐτῶν. Aq. and
Symm., ὡς ἀκρότομον πεφυτευμένην. Theod., εἰς πέτραν πεφυτευ-
μένοι οἱ υἱοὶ αὐτῆς. Vulgate, "Tyrus erat fundata." Syriac,
"Quemadmodum vidisti Tyrum." Targum, "Par erat
Tyro."

I will not love them any more,
All their princes are rebels.
16 Smitten is Ephraim,
Their root is dried up that fruit they shall not bring forth;
Even if they bear children,
I will slay the beloved of their womb.
17 My God shall reject them,
Because they have not hearkened to Him:
And they shall become wanderers among the nations.

## Chapter X.

1 A PRODUCTIVE vine (was) Israel,[1]
 (But) fruit it yields to itself;
 According to the increase of his fruit,
 He increased altars,
 According to the goodness of his land,
 He made good idol-statues.
2 He hath divided their heart;[2] now shall they be punished:
 He himself shall smite down their altars,
 He will destroy their idol-statues.
3 For now shall they say,
 There is no king to us;
 For we fear not Jehovah,
 And (as for) the king, what shall he do for us?
4 They speak (mere) words,
 They swear falsely (when) they make a covenant;[3]
 Therefore judgment springeth up like weeds

---

1. [1] "Productive," בוקק, (see versions.) The idea of productiveness, but not for God, referring to the radical meaning of Ephraim, seems to be uppermost in the prophet's mind.
 LXX., εὐκληματοῦσα. Aq., ἔνυδρος. Symm., ὑλομανοῦσα. Vulg., "Frondosa." Syr., "Vitis palmitum." Targum, "Vastata."

2. [2] "Divided." There is no reason why this word should not be thus rendered literally, if we regard it as a parallel passage to "God hardened Pharaoh's heart."

4. [3] This refers to their breaking faith with Shalmaneser, through entering into alliance with So, king of Egypt; the latter compact was a false oath.

Along the furrows of a field.
5 For the calves⁴ of Beth-aven,
The inhabitants of Samaria shall fear;
For its people shall mourn for it,
And its priests⁵ for it shall leap in agony,⁶
(Even) for its glory, because it is departed from it.⁷

5. ⁴ "For the calves," לעגלות. LXX., τῷ μόσχῳ τοῦ οἴκου Ὤν. Aq., τὰς δαμάλεις. Syr., "Vitulum Bethaven." Vulg., "Vaccas Bethaven." Targ., "Vitulos in Bethel."

⁵ "Priests," Chemarim, priests of Baal. Various derivations of this word have been suggested. Kimchi and Gesenius explain them as "black ones," from כמר, to "burn," be "scorched"—be "black," referring to the black dress worn by them. It would seem more likely, that as they were priests of the sun, the name was derived from the heat of that orb; they were those that were warm with the rays of their god—ever serving in his presence. The word occurs in two other places in Scripture, 2 Kings xxiii. 5, and Zeph. i. 4. In the former of these the LXX. has οἱ χωμαρίμ; in the latter, τῶν ἱερέων; in our passage, καθὼς παρεπίκραναν αὐτόν. The Vulgate has "Aruspices" in 2 Kings, and "Œditui" in the two other places. Newcome compares the Latin Camillus, the "Minister Flaminum."

⁶ "Leap in agony." It seems best to take יגילו in its primitive sense, "to leap," and not in its secondary sense, of "leaping with joy." Compare the actions of the priests of Baal when Elijah held his controversy with them, (1 Kings xviii. 26—28.) We have a prophecy here that these calves, the fruitful source of Israel's idolatry, should be taken away as spoil by the king of Assyria.

יגילו. LXX., ἐπιχαροῦνται. Vulg., "Exultaverunt." Syr., "Gestient." Targ., "Exultabant."

⁷ "From it," ממנו. LXX., ἀπ' αὐτοῦ. Syr. and Vulg., "Ab eo." Targ., "Ab eis."

6   Also as to itself, to Asshur it shall be carried,
    As an offering to the king that loves strife;[8]
    Shame shall Ephraim receive,
    And Israel shall blush at his own counsel.
7   Annihilated from Samaria is her king;
    Like the foam[9] on the face of the waters.
8   And destroyed shall be the high-places of Aven,
    The sin of Israel,
    The thorn and the thistle,
    Shall come up upon their altars;
    And they shall say to the mountains, Cover us,
    And to the hills, Fall on us.
9   Ever since the days of Gibeah,
    Hast thou sinned, O Israel;
    There they took their stand,
    The battle against the sons of iniquity
    Did not overtake them in Gibeah.[10]

6. [8] "Jareb." See note on chap. v. 13. ירב. LXX. and Syr. take this as a proper name. Aq., εἰκάζοντι. Symm., ὑπερμαχοῦντι. Vulgate, "Ultori." Targ., "Qui veniet punitum eos."

7. [9] "Foam," קצף. Interpreters differ much about this word. Symm., the Vulg., and the Targ. translate "foam," in which they are followed by the English version, and many modern commentators. The LXX. and Syr. and many critics of note, as Maurer, Delitzsch, &c., translate it "splinter," comparing קצפה, in Joel i. 7. After all that has been said, the figure of "foam" seems most appropriate, and may fairly be deduced from the same root, as the spray is a portion broken or separated from the water.

LXX., φρύγανον. Symm., ἐπίζεμα. Vulg., "Spumam," and so Targum. Syr., "Festucam."

9. [10] This verse seems to recall to mind the obstinacy of

10  My fixed-desire[11] is that I should punish them;
And that the peoples should be gathered against them,
When they are bound to their two iniquities.[12]
11  And Ephraim is a trained calf,
Accustomed to threshing,
Therefore I will mount
Upon her goodly neck;

Israel's wickedness in the days of old, (see Judges ch. xix. and xx.) They stood persistently, yet God spared them from extinction, the battle did not utterly destroy them, but now the visitation for impenitence and idolatry shall be more sharp and severe.

10. [11] "My fixed-desire," באותי. The LXX. derived this word from בוא, and rendered ἦλθε, (so the Alexandrian MS.) Many moderns have adopted this derivation. It is better, however, to keep to the Hebrew text. The ב is the *beth essentiæ*, which is expressed by the addition of the word "fixed."

Vulg., "Juxta desiderium meum." Sym., "In correptione meâ."

[12] "Two iniquities." Various have been the interpretations of this word, עינתם. The K'ri and many MSS. read עונתם, their "iniquities." Some have suggested that it should be translated "eyes"—"before their eyes"—but עינים is always used to express a person's "eyes." Others, as the Chaldee and English version, explain it as "furrows." Again, when the choice of translation has been made, a great difference of opinion exists as to the allusion—if "furrows," the reference may be to the two divisions of the nation, that both Israel and Judah had turned to their own way; or Dan and Bethel may be thus designated, as the two head-quarters of the calf-worship. If "iniquities," which seems the preferable reading, the reference may be, as Delitzsch thinks, to the

I will ride on Ephraim, Judah shall plough,
Jacob shall harrow for himself.

12 Sow to yourselves for righteousness,
Reap ye according to piety,
Break for you the fallow-field;
It is time also to seek Jehovah,
Until He come,
And teach righteousness[13] to you.

13 Ye have ploughed wickedness,
Iniquity ye have reaped,
Ye have eaten the fruit of lies;
Because thou trustedst in thy way,[14]
In the multitude of thy mighty ones.

---

forsaking of Jehovah and David their king; or, which is more natural and agreeable to the context, the two calves by which Jeroboam had made Israel to sin.
LXX., ταῖς δυσὶν ἀδικίαις αὐτῶν. Syr., "Duas stultitias suas." Vulg., "Duas iniquitates suas." Targ., "Ad duos sulcos."

12. [13] "Teach righteousness." Not as in English version and Delitzsch, "rain righteousness." This is a clear Messianic prophecy, (see Joel ii. 23, and a valuable comment in Hengstenberg's "Christology," vol. ii. p. 319.) Compare the constant use of διδάσκαλος, "master" or "teacher," as a title of our Lord in the Gospels, and the word "Maran," derived from this root, in 1 Cor. xvi. 22.
LXX., ἕως τοῦ ἐλθεῖν γεννήματα δικαιοσύνης. Syr., "Ostendat vobis justitiam suam." Vulg., "Cum venerit qui docebit vos justitiam." Targ., "Adferet vobis justitiam."

13. [14] "In thy way," בדרכך. LXX., ἐν ἅρμασί σου, reading ברכבך. A reading supported by many authorities. Syr., Targ., and Vulg. follow the Hebrew text, "in viis."

## CHAPTER X.    65

14  And there shall arise¹⁵ a tumult among thy tribes,
    And all thy strongholds shall be destroyed,
    According as Shalman¹⁶ destroyed Beth-arbel¹⁷ in
      the day of battle ;
    The mother on the children was dashed in pieces.
15  Even thus hath he done to you, O (inhabitants
      of) Bethel,
    Because of the wickedness of your wickedness ;
    In the morning¹⁸
    Utterly annihilated shall be the king of Israel.

14. ¹⁵ וקאם. א is a *mater lectionis.* Compare כארי in Ps. xxii. 16.

¹⁶ Shalman, *i.e.*, Shalmaneser ; it would appear from this passage, that this prophecy was uttered between the two expeditions of Shalmaneser.

¹⁷ Beth-arbel is probably Arbela in Upper Galilee, (1 Macc. ix. 2.) The LXX., instead of Beth-arbel, ἐκ τοῦ οἴκου τοῦ Ἱεροβοάμ. And the Alex. MS., Ἱεροβαάλ, *i.e.*, Gideon. Vulg., " A domo ejus qui judicavit Baal." Syr., " Salma—Bethil." Targ., בכמנא שלמא, " Pacificus per insidias."

15. ¹⁸ " In the morning," בשחר. Several MSS. read כ, instead of ב, כשחר, " like the morning." So Vulg., " Sicut mane." The king referred to is Hoshea.

F

## Chapter XI.

1 Because[1] Israel was a child, therefore I loved him:
And out of Egypt I called my son.[2]

1. [1] "Because." All the ancient versions, it will be seen, translate כי thus; the Targum only has "when;" and the Syriac seems to combine the two ideas of the ground of love and the time.

[2] "My son." (See Ex. iv. 22, 23.) As Israel was the nation of which Messiah should come according to the flesh, that nation contained the germ of the humanity of Christ. Accordingly we sometimes find an interchange of names and epithets between the king and the kingdom, the things proper to the type are predicated of the antitype; the head and the members are viewed as one, or at least inseparable. Thus in Isaiah xlix. 3, Messiah is again called "Israel." And so St. Matthew applies the passage—as Israel in her infancy as a nation was brought out of Egypt, so it was with Israel's infant King. The same country provided a cradle for both, and both were led up from the same land to be a witness for God before the world. Bengel's suggestion (see Gnomon Nov. Test., in Matt. ii. 15) is worth attention, though it may not carry conviction; he takes the מ, "from," in ממצרים, "from Egypt," as referring to time and not to place: "From the time that Israel was in Egypt, I called him my son." And he argues that St. Matthew applies the words to Messiah in the same sense, viz., to His sojourn in Egypt, rather than His return from Egypt; that from His very nativity He was the Son of God; and that soon after His birth He was in Egypt, and so from the first God recognised the Sonship of Messiah. The whole passage, however, rather pictures to us the feebleness of the nation in the midst of foes, and God's love in delivering them, tending them in the wilderness, and educating them to be a special people for Himself.

The renderings of this verse by the versions are—LXX.,

2  They called³ them;
   Surely they went from their presence,
   To Baalim they sacrifice,
   And to graven images they burn incense.

ὅτι νήπιος Ἰσραήλ, καὶ ἐγὼ ἠγάπησα αὐτὸν, καὶ ἐξ Αἰγύπτου μετεκάλεσα τὰ τέκνα αὐτοῦ. Aquila, ὅτι παῖς Ἰσραήλ, καὶ ἠγάπησα αὐτὸν, καὶ ἀπὸ Αἰγύπτου ἐκάλεσα τὸν υἱόν μου. Symm., ὅτι παῖς Ἰσραήλ καὶ ἠγαπημένος, ἐξ Αἰγύπτου κέκληται υἱός μου. Theod., ὅτι νήπιος Ἰσραήλ, καὶ ἠγάπησα αὐτὸν, καὶ ἐκάλεσα υἱόν μου ἐξ Αἰγύπτου. Vulg., "Quia puer Israel, et dilexi eum; et ex Egypto vocavi filium meum." Syr., "Quia dum puer esset Israel, dilexi eum, et inde ab Egypto vocavi eum filium meum." Targ., "Quando puer erat Israel, diligebam eum, et ex Egypto vocavi eos filios."

2. ³ "They called," קראו. This is one of the most difficult amongst the many difficult passages in our prophet. What is the nominative to the verb קראו, "they called?" who are the "they?" Some reply the Egyptians, and render "they called them," *i.e.*, back, yet "surely they went from them." The LXX., which is followed by a large class of commentators, read the verb in the first person, and the suffix attached to the word "presence" in the same, and interpret, "I (God) called them, so they departed from my presence." The ancient versions subjoined will show that the same difficulty existed in their day as in our own; and apparently they had recourse to a method which still finds favour with many, they cut the knot by altering the text. The more difficult reading, as a rule, is much more likely to be the true one than the easier. If the verb had been originally in the first person singular, no one could have changed it into the third person plural, thus introducing a flood of difficulty. Moreover, the fact that the Alexandrine MS. of LXX. reads the verb in the third person singular, proves that the easy mode of escape was an invention. The interpretation of the Targum has much to recommend it. "They," *i.e.*, the

3   And I myself taught Ephraim to walk,[4]
    Taking them by their arms;
    But they knew not that I healed them.
4   With the cords of man[5] I drew them, with the
      bands of love;
    And I was to them the remover[6] of the yoke (that
      pressed) upon their cheeks;
    And I held out[7] to him (food), I made him eat.

prophets, "called them," but they fled from their presence and sacrificed to idols. The third person plural, according to a frequent use, will then simply refer to those whose duty it was, as commissioned of God, to communicate His will to Israel—in the first place Moses and Aaron, and after them all the servants of God who were sent to recover and reform the rebellious people.

LXX., μετεκάλεσα (some MSS. μετεκαλέσατο) αὐτοὺς οὕτως ἀπῴχοντο ἐκ προσώπου μου. Syr., "Vocaverunt eos, sic abierunt a conspectu meo." Vulg., "Vocaverunt eos ita abierunt a facie eorum." Targ., "Misi prophetas meos ut erudirent eos illorum conspectum."

3. [4] "I taught Ephraim to walk." After I had brought Israel out of Egypt, which deliverance was the national birth of the people, I reared and trained them as a nurse does a child. Taking this passage in connection with Deut. i. 31, we have a strong support for the reading ἐτροφοφόρησεν, in Acts xiii. 18. This is the reading of the Alexandrine MS., whereas ἐτροποφόρησεν, followed by the English version, is supported by the Sinaitic, Vatican, and Beza's MSS., and the Vulgate.

4. [5] "With the cords of man," בחבלי אדם. LXX., ἐν διαφθορᾷ ἀνθρώπων. Aq., Symm., and Theod., "In funiculis hominum." Vulg., "In funiculis Adam."

[6] The כ in כמרימי, is the particle of assertion. For the doctrine of the passage, see Matt. xi. 30.

[7] "I held out." וְאַט, fut. apoc. Hiphil of נטה. So Symm.

5 He shall not return to the land of Egypt,
  But it is Asshur (that shall be) his king;
  Because they refused to return (to me).
6 And brandished shall the sword be in his cities,
  And shall consume his defenders[8] and devour (them);
  Because of their counsels.
7 And my people (shall be) in doubt about their revolting from me,[9]

and Syr. Delitzsch and Fürst regard it as the adverb "gently," (see 2 Sam. xviii. 5.)

In the LXX., the latter part of this verse reads καὶ ἔσομαι αὐτοῖς ὡς ῥαπίζων ἄνθρωπος ἐπὶ τὰς σιαγόνας αὐτοῦ. Καὶ ἐμβλέψομαι πρὸς αὐτόν, ευνήσομαι αὐτῷ. Symm., "Et putaverunt quod imponerem jugum super maxillam eorum, et declinavi ad eum cibos." Vulg., "Et ero eis quasi exaltans jugum super maxillas eorum: et declinavi ad eum ut vesceretur." The Syriac and Targ. support the Hebrew text.

5. From 2 Kings xvii. 4, we learn that king Hoshea secretly conspired against the king of Assyria, and sent messengers to So, king of Egypt; and this treachery seems to have brought on the final catastrophe of Samaria. This alliance with Egypt is the matter under reproof and rebuke in this verse.

6. [8] "Defenders," בדים, literally, "bars" or "barriers;" used here for the idols whom they had chosen for their defence, and trusted in as a shield or a stronghold, (see ch. iv. 18.)

בדיו. LXX., ἐν ταῖς χερσὶν αὐτοῦ. Symm., "Brachia illius." Vulg., "Electos ejus." Syr., "E manibus." Targ., "Proceres."

7. [9] This clause, ועמי תלואים למשובתי, has been differently rendered:—

"My people are bent on apostacy from me."—*Keil and Delitzsch.*

And to the High One[10] shall they cry,
He shall not at all lift them up.
8 How shall I yield thee, O Ephraim,
(How) abandon[11] thee, O Israel,
How yield thee as Admah,
(How) set thee as Zeboim?
Changed in me is my heart,
Altogether stirred up are my compassions.
9 I will not accomplish the heat of my wrath,

"My people shall hang in doubt, because of their turning away from me."—*Newcome*.
"My people shall hang in anxious suspense till my returning."—*Horsley*.
Hengstenberg, "Veracity of the Pentateuch," vol. i., p. 127, has pointed out the connection between this passage and Deut. xxviii. 66, the only two places where this verb is spelt with the א. This reference is clear, and the sense is, "My people shall be in doubt and anxiety, as the consequence of apostacy from me"—the suffix being objective, as is frequently the case.
LXX., καὶ ὁ λαὸς αὐτοῦ ἐπικρεμάμενος ἐκ τῆς κατοικίας αὐτοῦ. Syr., "Populus meus hæsitat in redeundo." Vulg., "Populus meus pendebit ad reditum meum." Targ., "Populus meus hæsitat se convertere."
[10] "High One," על. See ch. vii. 16, for the different interpretations of this difficult word.
LXX., ὁ Θεός. So also Syr. Vulg., "Jugum." Targ., "In infirmitatem gravem."
8. [11] "Abandon," אמגנך. The word is used here in the same sense as in Gen. xiv. 20. The old versions mostly took it in the sense of "shielding," connecting it with מגן.
LXX., ὑπερασπιῶ σου. Aq., ὅπλῳ κυκλώσω σε. Symm., ἐκτείσω σε. Theod., ἀφοπλίζω σε. Vulg., "Protegam te." Syr., "Juvarem te." Targ., "Exterminabo te."

I will not return to destroy Ephraim;
For God am I, and not man,
In the midst of thee the Holy One,
Therefore I will not come against the city.¹²
10 After Jehovah shall they go,
As a lion He shall roar;
When He shall roar,
Then shall (His) sons flutter from the west.
11 They shall flutter like a sparrow from Egypt,
And like a dove from the land of Asshur;
And I will make them dwell in their own houses,
Declareth Jehovah.

9. ¹² "Against the city." I am the Holy One in the midst of thee; I will not come against my dwelling-place. This seems to be the meaning of this passage. All the ancient versions read thus. בעיר is generally, however, interpreted "in wrath," from עור. Fürst gives both renderings of this passage. Vitringa has suggested a clever escape from the difficulty—by reading כעיר, (or perhaps as in text, בעיר, taking ב as *beth essentiæ*,) and rendering, "as an enemy," ער = עיר.

בעיר. LXX., εἰς πόλιν. And so Syr., "Urbem." Vulg., "Civitatem." And so Targ.

10. בנים מים. LXX., τέκνα ὑδάτων. Vulg., "Filii maris." Syr., "Pavebunt filii populum." Targ., "Ab occidente."

## Chapter XII.

1  Surrounded me with lies hath Ephraim,
   And with deceit the house of Israel;
   And as for Judah, he moreover strayeth[1] from[2] God,
   And from the Holy One[3] (who is) faithful.[4]
2  Ephraim feedeth on wind,

1. [1] "Strayeth," רד. The rabbies derived this word from רדה, "to rule," hence this translation is found in Luther and the English version. The Vulgate reads "descendit," as if from ירד. Modern critics derive the word from רוד, "to ramble" or "stray." (Comp. Gen. xxvii. 40; Ps. lv. 3; Jer. ii. 31.) The context in the third verse shows that this meaning is not only more correct grammatically, but is the only consistent one.

[2] "From," literally, "with," עם, *i.e.*, "from with," מעם. The leading idea is that of reference—gone astray with reference to God.

[3] "Holy One," קדושים, literally, "Holy ones"—a plural title of God, as in Josh. xxiv. 19; Prov. ix. 10. Plural nouns and adjectives are frequently attributed to God, (see Ps. lxxviii. 25; Mal. i. 6, &c.

[4] "Faithful," נאמן, is singular, referring nevertheless to "Holy Ones" (see, for similar example, Ps. vii. 10.) Mark the accumulation of the attributes of God—"God the mighty," אל; "God the Holy," קדושים; "God the faithful," נאמן.

The rendering of this difficult verse is thus given by the ancient authorities:—LXX., καὶ Ἰούδα νῦν ἔγνω αὐτοὺς ὁ Θεός, καὶ ὁ λαὸς ἅγιος κληθήσεται Θεοῦ. Syr., "Donec descenderet populus dei, populus sanctus et fidelis." Vulg., "Testis descendit cum Deo, et cum sanctis fidelis." Targ., "Validi fuerunt,—vocantur populus sanctus in eo quod fuerunt stabiles." Aq. renders רד, by ἐπικράτει.

2. Hoshea, the king of the ten tribes, had made a covenant

## CHAPTER XII.

And pursueth the east wind,
All the day long,
Lying and violence he multiplieth;
And a covenant with Asshur they make,
And oil to Egypt is carried.
3 And Jehovah hath a strife with Judah;
And He will visit upon Jacob according to his ways,
According to his actions He will requite him.
4 In the womb he supplanted his brother;[5]
And in his maturity he prevailed with God.

with Assyria, and yet sent into Egypt for help against them; this is the lie referred to, (see 2 Kings xvii. 4.)

4. [5] The illustration that follows from the faith and practice of their father Jacob, conveys a lesson of instruction and rebuke to them. When Jacob, who had a token of his future superiority over his brother from the womb, was in after years in deep distress and terror at the thought of meeting Esau, he had recourse to prayer and confidence in God and His promises, and his petition was granted. So, in the midst of their present disasters, his descendants also should betake themselves unto the same never-failing refuge, remembering the promises that God had given them. Assyria, like Esau, might be an object of fear; but instead of seeking heathen aid, they should "wait on their God continually." Again, Jacob, in banishment in Syria, tended Laban's sheep, and laboured hard for a wife of his own family and faith, that he might not be ensnared by an idolatrous alliance, and as a reward his posterity were brought up out of Egypt by Moses, as a flock under the guidance of a shepherd; and so they should not make league with Egypt, but rely upon their God, and He would give them the same deliverance that He had vouchsafed to their forefathers.

5   And he prevailed with the Angel⁶ and overcame,
    He wept, and prayed to Him;
    At Bethel He found him,
    And (it was) there He spake with us.⁷
6   Even Jehovah,⁸ God of Sabaoth;⁹
    Jehovah (is) his memorial.

5.  ⁶ "Angel"—the Logos, the Mediator, the second person in the Trinity. For an exhaustive article on the subject of the "Angel of Jehovah," see Hengstenberg's "Christology," vol. iv., p. 285, where he shows (1) that מלאך, "angel," is derived from a root, לאך, "to work;" the Angel of the Lord is He who operates, reveals, declares, carries on the government of the Father; (2) that the expressions מלאך האלהים and מלאך יהוה, can only be rendered "*the* angel of God," "*the* angel of Jehovah," and not "*an* angel," as when two nouns stand together and each of them is definite, the article is only prefixed to the second, and when a proper name or pronoun stands as the second, it has the same force as a noun with the article. (See also Dr. M'Caul's treatise on the same subject, in Kimchi's commentary on Zechariah.)

⁷ "With us," עמנו, LXX., πρὸς αὐτούς. Aquila, Symm., Theod., and Syr., "With him." Vulg., "Vobiscum."

6.  ⁸ "Jehovah." Mark that the Angel is here distinctly called by this incommunicable name, (see also Ex. iii., the basis of this passage, in which the Angel and Jehovah, or God, are spoken of as one.) Volumes have been written on this title. The chief points to be noted are these:— יהוה is clearly derived from היה, "to be;" the Rabbies regard it as embodying the three tensic forms of the verb—היה, "He was;" הוה, "being," or "He is;" and יהיה, "He shall be." This seems referred to by St. John, Rev. i. 8, ὁ ὢν καὶ ὁ ἦν καὶ ὁ ἐρχόμενος, "He that is, and that was, and that is to come;" and Heb. xiii. 8, "Jesus Christ, the same yesterday,

7 Therefore do thou to thy God return,
   Piety and judgment keep,
   And hope in thy God continually.

to-day, and for ever." Modern critics take the word to be the old future form of the verb, יִהְיֶה, or יַהְוֶה, "He shall be," or in an indefinite sense, "He is." The expanded form is given us in Ex. iii. 14, אֶהְיֶה אֲשֶׁר אֶהְיֶה, " I am who am," *i.e.*, the self-existent. LXX., ἐγώ εἰμι ὁ ὤν. Vulg., "Ego sum qui sum." Others have insisted on the strictly future sense of the word, "He shall be," and compare with it the New Testament, ὁ ἐρχόμενος, "He that should come." (See, for able articles on the subject, Hengstenberg's "Veracity of the Pentateuch," Smith's "Dictionary of the Bible," &c.)

9 "Sabaoth." There is much difficulty in explaining this word—more familiar in its translated form, "hosts."

(1) It may be that all created worlds—the armies of the skies—are intended. This is clearly the meaning of the word where it occurs for the first time, (Gen. ii. 1.)

(2) It may refer to the armies of Israel, which are called, Ex. xii. 41, צבאות יהוה, "the hosts of the LORD."

(3) It may comprehend both; in the sense that whatever things are created, whatever powers there be, whether in heaven or in earth, material or immaterial, angelic or human, Jehovah is the God of them all.

(4) It may be a title of God, in apposition to the other name or names with which it stands associated, explanatory of the executive omnipotency of the Divine Being—as "Elohim" represents the concentration and seat of all powers, so "Sabaoth" all the manifestations of the majesty and mightiness of God. The reader will not fail to note that all these titles of deity are here attributed to the Angel of the Covenant, of whom Jacob said in the ground-text of our passage, "I have seen God," (Gen. xxxii. 30.) It is worthy of remark that the title, "LORD of Hosts," is not found in the books of Moses, Joshua, Judges, or Ruth. It first appears in

8   Canaan![10]
    In his hand are balances of deceit;
    To oppress he loves.
9   Then said Ephraim,
    Surely I have waxed rich,
    I have acquired wealth for myself;
    In all my labours,
    They shall not find in me
    Iniquity which is sin.[11]
10  But I myself am Jehovah thy God,
    From the land of Egypt;
    Again I will make thee dwell in tents
    As in the days of the festival.
11  And I spoke to the prophets,
    And I myself the vision multiplied;
    And by means of the prophets I uttered
        parables.             [lit., *by the hand*]
12  Surely Gilead is iniquity;
    Yea, vanity[12] have they become:
    In Gilgal, oxen they sacrifice,

the books of Samuel. It is twice found in the New Testament in its untranslated form, (Rom. ix. 29; Jas. v. 4.)

8.  [10] "Canaan." A striking apostrophe. Not Israel, but Canaan; not a prince with God, but a dishonest merchant, degenerated into the evil practices of those he was commissioned to destroy.

9.  [11] That is, wrongdoing, specially with reference to idolatry and the gains which accrued to them through alliance with heathen nations, which can be charged as deserving punishment.

12. [12] "Iniquity," און, and "vanity," שוא, refer to the idols of the place. (See ch. vi. 8.)

## CHAPTER XII.

Also their altars are like heaps,[13]
On the furrows of the field.
13 And Jacob fled to the field of Aram;
And Israel toiled for a wife,
And for a wife he tended (sheep).
14 And by a prophet,[14]
Jehovah brought up Israel from Egypt;
And by a prophet, was he tended.
15 Ephraim hath provoked most bitterly;
   [lit., *bitternesses*]
And his blood upon him his Lord[15] shall leave,
And his disgrace shall requite unto him.

[13] "Heaps," בלים. The suitability of this figure will be apparent when it is remembered that Gilead, or Galeed, *i.e.*, "the heap of witness," was the place where Jacob and Laban made covenant with each other, (see Gen. xxxi. 47,) and Gilgal the place where the heap of stones taken from the river's bed was set up for a memorial of the passage of Jordan, (Josh. iv. 19—24,) and where the people renewed their allegiance to the Lord by the rite of circumcision, and where the Lord rolled away the reproach of Egypt from them, (Josh. v. 2—9;) but now, alas! in these very places, the altars dedicated to their idols are like heaps on the furrows of the field.

14. [14] "A prophet." Moses. (See Deut. xviii. 15.)

15. [15] "His Lord" is the subject of both the verbs, "leave" and "requite." God's calling of Jacob and the patriarch's simple reliance upon God throughout his career, are brought into sharp contrast throughout this chapter with the unbelief and degeneracy of his posterity.

## Chapter XIII.

1 When Ephraim spoke, (there was) reverence,[1]
  He exalted himself in Israel;
  But he became guilty with Baal and died.
2 And now they sin yet more, [lit., *add to sin*]
  And make for them a cast,
  Out of their silver, by their skill (they make) idols,
  The work of smiths it is entirely!
  To the people they say, [lit., *to them*]
  (Even) the men who sacrifice,[2]
  The calves let (the crowds) adore.

1 [1] "There was reverence," רתת. This is the only place where this word occurs; its interpretation is consequently very difficult. It is generally referred to the Aramæan, רתט, (Jer. xlix. 24,) by most commentators, ancient and modern. Hengstenberg translates the passage, "When Ephraim uttered perversity, then he bore his sin in Israel," &c.
LXX., κατὰ τὸν λόγον 'Εφραὶμ δικαιώματα ἔλαβεν αὐτὸς ἐν τῷ 'Ισραήλ, καὶ ἔθετο αὐτὰ τῇ βάαλ καὶ ἀπέθανε. Aq., φρίκην ἔλαβεν αὐτός. Symm. and Theod., "Tremorem." Vulg., "Loquente Ephraim, horror invasit Israel." Syr., "Dum loqueretur Deus, Aphrem tremebat." Targ., "Cum loquitur nonnullus de domo Ephraim tremor apprehendit populos."

2. [2] "Men who sacrifice"—literally, "sacrificers of men;" which may either mean those who offer human sacrifices—this view is taken by the LXX., Vulg., and many Jewish and Christian critics—or, "those of them who are appointed to offer sacrifices," (see, for the same construction, Isa. xxix. 19; Micah v. 4.) This latter interpretation is to be preferred, as human sacrifices were not offered to Baal. The sense of the passage is this, they made a calf, and those men whose office is to sacrifice, *i.e.*, the idolatrous priests, say, "Let the people

## CHAPTER XIII. 79

3   Therefore shall they be like a cloud of the morning,
    And like dew which goes early away,
    As chaff which is whirled from the floor,
    And as smoke from the loop-hole.³
4   But I myself (am) Jehovah thy God,
    From the land of Egypt;
    And a God besides me thou knewest not,
    And no other Saviour (was there) but myself.
5   I knew thee in the wilderness,
    In the land of (great) drought       [*droughts*]
6   According to their pasture,⁴ so were they satisfied;

worship the calves"— "worship," literally, " kiss "—this throws ridicule and satire on their folly.

LXX., Ἀυτοὶ λέγουσι Θύσατε ἀνθρώπους, μόσχοι γὰρ ἐκλελοίπασι. Aq., μόσχους καταφιλοῦντες. Symm., " Immolate, homines vitulos adorate," μόσχους προσκυνήσατε. Vulg., " His ipsi dicunt immolate homines vitulos adorantes." Syr., " Dicebant eis prophetæ, O qui sacrificatis homines et vitulum osculamini." Targ., " Pseudoprophetæ sacra celebrant operi manuum hominis, boves immolant vitulis."

3. ³ " Loop-hole," or "window." The houses having no chimneys, the smoke made its escape by the lattice or orifice, which served the double purpose of emitting the smoke and admitting light.

מגרן — כמץ. LXX., ὡς χνοῦς—ἀφ' ἄλωνος. The other versions, ὡς ἀράχνη—λαίλαπι. Vulg., " Pulvis ex area." And similarly Syr. and Targ.

וכעשן מארבה. LXX., καὶ ὡς ἀτμὶς ἀπὸ δακρύων. Theod., ἀπὸ καπνοδόκης. Symm., " De foramine." Syr., " Fumus e fenestra." Vulg., " Sicut fumus de fumario," and so Targum.

6. ⁴ " According as they were fed," כמרעיתם. LXX., κατὰ τὰς νομὰς αὐτῶν. Symm., κατὰ τὴν νομὴν αὐτῶν. Vulg.,

Satisfied they were, and lifted up was their heart;
Therefore have they forgotten me.
7 And I will be to them like a lion;
Like a leopard by the way-side I will lurk.[5]
8 I will meet them like a bear bereaved (of her cubs),
And I will tear the caul of their heart;
And I will devour them there like a lioness,
The beast of the field shall tear them.
9 The destruction (is) thine own,[6] O Israel,
But I am thy (true) help.

"Juxta pascua sua." Syr. regards it as a verb, "Pavi eos." Targ., "Enutrivi eos."

7. [5] "Lurk," אָשׁוּר, from שׁוּר, "to watch." Several MSS., LXX., Vulgate, Syriac, and Arabic, read אַשּׁוּר, "to Assyria." The Targum renders "insidiatur." Delitzsch well remarks that from this point the verbs are in the indefinite tense, because the punishments were already begun.

9 [6] "The destruction (is) thine own." Regarding שחת as a noun. The song that Moses taught the children of Israel (Deut. xxxii.) seems to have been present to the prophet's mind. In verse 5 of that chapter we meet with the word שחת לו, applied to the corrupt and destructive doings of the perverse generation, whose disgrace it was that they were not God's children. The second part of our verse contains a reference to Deut. xxxiii. 26 — "There is none like the God of Jeshurun, who rideth on the heaven in thy help," rather, "as thy help," בעזרך. This ground-text explains the force of ב, here not "against," as most modern critics have rendered it, but rather as the Beth of emphasis. It is best also to take the ב in בי, as having the same force. The two prepositions are employed to give a special force to the assertion, "The

## CHAPTER XIII. 81

10 Where⁷ is thy king. prithee,

                    [or, *I will be thy king.*]
To save thee in all thy cities;
And (where are) thy judges,
Of whom thou saidst,
Give me a king and princes.

11 I give⁸ thee a king in my anger,
And take (him) away in my outbursting wrath.

destruction which thou art suffering is all thy own. It is I, and I only, that am thy real helper."

LXX., τῇ διαφθορᾷ σου Ἰσραήλ τίς βοηθήσει. Syr., "Perdidi te, O Israel, quis auxiliaretur tibi." Vulg., "Perditio tua, Israel, tantummodo in me auxilium tuum." Targum, "Vos depravatis—O domus Israel—Verbum meum fuit vobis præsidio."

10. ⁷ "Where." The English version takes this word, אהי, to be the future of היה, "I will be," but renders in the margin, "where." This translation yields no sense, and is in violation of the accents, as it connects אהי with the following word, which is separated from it by the accent Zakeph-katon. It is better to translate the word, with most modern critics, "where," regarding it as a variety of אי or איה. The form אהי only occurs in this place and twice in verse 14. אפוא is like the Greek ποτέ and Latin "tandem"—"prithee."

אהי. LXX., ποῦ. Vulg., "Ubi." And so Syriac and Targum.

11. ⁸ "I give," אתן, and "I took away," אקח. The use of the future or indefinite tense here implies that this giving and removing of their king was a continued act on the part of God. Not only does the statement call to mind the Divine dealings with Saul, but probably the thought uppermost in the prophet's mind was the violent death that had befallen so many of Israel's kings at this

G

12  Stored up is the iniquity of Ephraim,
    Treasured is his sin.
13  The pangs of a travailing woman shall come upon him;
    He is a son by no means wise,
    For he should not linger a long time,
    Whilst in the act of being born.[9]
14  From the hand of Hades I will redeem[10] them,
    From death I will avenge them;
    Where[11] (are) thy plagues, O death,
    Where thy sting, O Hades,
    Compassion (on them) shall be hid from my eyes.

period. Zachariah had been murdered by Shallum, Shallum by Menahem, Pekahiah by Pekah, and Pekah by Hoshea, who was now on the eve of being carried away captive by the king of Assyria.

12. See Deut. xxxii. 34.

13. [9] The sense of this verse is that as conversion is compared to a new birth, both in the individual (see John iii. 3) and in the whole creation, (see Matt. xxiv. 8, orig.,) so after all the judgments that have been poured out on Ephraim to bring about his conversion to God, he ought not to linger in the course of regeneration, but hasten to enter into life, the new life of a restored and reconciled child of God.

14. [10] "Redeem," פדה, "avenge," גאל. The first verb refers to redemption by purchase, the second to redemption by avengement. The one represents the right, the second the assertion of the right. Christ was the Redeemer of His people, פדה, on the cross; He will be their Avenger, גאל, at His second coming.

[11] "Where." This is the same word as in verse 10. The LXX., Aquila, Syr., E., and Arabic, backed up by the quotation by St. Paul, 1 Cor. xv. 55, take this word as

15  Though he amongst (his) brethren be fruitful,[12]
There shall come an east wind, a wind of Jehovah,
From the wilderness arising,

stated above, (verse 10,) in the sense of "where." The Vulgate, Symm., and English version, supported by Targum, as the future of the verb היה, "to be," "I will be." One thing seems certain, that the same meaning must belong to the word here as in the tenth verse, and as no other meaning but "where" will suit the context there, so it seems right to conclude that this is the true interpretation in both places. There is a chronological connection between the restoration of Israel and the resurrection of the dead, (see Dan. xii. 1, 2 ;) hence we may trace one out of many causes for the employment of language which may refer to either or include both.

אחי. LXX ποῦ ἡ δίκη σου. Aquila and E., ποῦ εἰσιν οἱ λόγοι σου. Symm. ἔσομαι πληγή σου. Vulg., "Ero mors tua, O mors, morsus tuus ero inferne." Syr., "Ubi victoria,—ubi stimulus." Targ., "Mox erit verbum meum contra eos in necem."

15.  [12] "Be fruitful," פריא. An irony upon the name of Ephraim = "fruitful."

With this and the following verse, which should not be separated by the division of the chapters, end the prophecies of judgment. The roll written within and without with lamentation, and mourning, and woe, is here closed. Soon after these words had fallen from the prophet's lips, Shalmaneser came up like a desolating blast, and besieged Samaria, 723 B.C., and the blockade lasted till 721 B.C. Then the fountain of Ephraim was dried up, and Samaria fell. Ever since that day the ten-tribe kingdom has been obliterated and lost; either absorbed (as is most likely the case) into the tribe of Judah, or awaiting some special interposition on the part of God to manifest them to the world. Under any circumstances the dirge

And shall parch up his fountain,
And dried up shall be his spring,
He[13] shall plunder the treasure of all (his) well-loved goods. [lit., *goods of desire*]

of "judgment" now gives place to the "song of mercy;" and as the predicted punishment has been executed, we look forward in faith grounded on that very fact, and on the faithfulness of our God, that the predicted conversion and restoration of Israel will not fail of fulfilment. Like the body of their lawgiver, no man knows of their sepulchre, but like him, in the day when this fallen world shall be clothed again with glory from above, and the kingdom established, they also shall be seen upon the mount of transfiguration, restored and reconciled under their king Messiah.

[13] "He," that is, Shalmaneser, the subject of the figure in the foregoing part of the verse.

## Chapter XIV.

1 Punished shall be Samaria,
   Because she hath rebelled against her God;
   By the sword shall they fall,
   Their babes shall be dashed in pieces,
   And their pregnant women be ripped up.
2 Be converted, O Israel,
   To¹ Jehovah thy God;
   For thou hast fallen by thine own iniquity.
3 Take with you words,²
   And be converted to Jehovah;
   Say unto Him, all (our) iniquity forgive,
   And receive (us), O Gracious One,³

---

2. ¹ " *To* Jehovah," &c. עַד, " up to," not merely אֶל, " towards." The summons to conversion is not merely one of direction, but of completion.

3. ² " Words." The open confession of sins, and the utterance of prayer out of the fulness of a penitent and broken heart.

³ " Receive (us), O Gracious One." The ordinary view of this passage is that it contains a prayer to God to receive the only good thing that the returning sinner can offer, namely, penitence and confession; but surely there is a reference here to chap. iii. 5:—

> " They shall seek Jehovah their God,
>   And David their king,
>   And revere Jehovah
>   And His Gracious One
>   In the last days."

And we will repay (as) heifers[4] our lips.

4 Asshur shall not save us,
On horses we will not ride,
And we will not say any more
"O our gods," to the work of our hands;[5]

This prophecy is here regarded as fulfilled, or on the threshold of fulfilment; whatever therefore is the meaning of טובו in the former passage, must be the meaning of טוב in this. We have stated that the parallelism in that place requires us to regard "His Gracious One," as synonymous with "David their king," *i.e.*, the Messiah, and it seems best, consequently, to understand it so here. For the construction, &c., compare Ps. xxxiv. 12, (see also note on chap. iii. 5.) It may, however, be urged for the ordinary view, that the writer of the Epistle to the Hebrews, (ch. xiii. 15,) after referring to this passage according to the LXX., adds, "But to do *good* and to communicate, forget not, for with such *sacrifices* God is well pleased," which looks very much like a continuance of the reference to this passage.

[4] "Heifers," &c. We will bring the offerings of penitence and prayer, like sacrifices, to the altar. In Heb. xiii. 15, we find this verse quoted from the LXX., καρπὸν χειλέων, as if they had read פְּרִי, "fruit," instead of פָּרִים, "heifers." LXX., εἴπατε αὐτῷ ὅπως μὴ λάβητε ἀδικίαν καὶ λάβητε ἀγαθά, καὶ ἀνταποδώσομεν καρπὸν χειλέων ἡμῶν. Vulg., "Et dicite ei : omnem aufer iniquitatem, accipe bonum : et reddemus vitulos labiorum nostrorum." Syr., "Dicite illi ut dimittat vobis iniquitatem vestram, et bona suscipite; rependet enim vobis fructus labiorum vestrorum." Targum, "Suscipiamur quasi boni et sint eloquia tanquam boves," &c.

4. [5] Israel here confesses and renounces her most prominent sins, dependence on Assyria and Egypt, the latter being referred to in "the horses," (see Deut. xvii. 16,) and idolatry, and then casts herself on the mercy of her covenant

## CHAPTER XIV.

      Because by Thee pitied shall be the orphan.[6]
5  I will heal their revolting,
    I will love them gratuitously;
    For turned aside is my anger from him.

                              [i.e., *Israel.*]

God, and pleads His pity and grace to the poor and destitute orphan.

> "Nothing in my hand I bring,
> Simply to Thy cross I cling."

[6] "Pitied shall be the orphan." יֻרְחַם is from the same verb as the name Lo-Ruhamah, the female infant of Gomer, by which the utter feebleness and helplessness of Israel was pourtrayed, (ch. i. 6;) but now the time was come when the change of that name from Lo-Ruhamah to Ruhamah (ch. ii. 3) had arrived, so we read here that the orphan race of Israel finds mercy from the Lord. This word, יֻרְחַם, thus serves as a key to unlock the mystery of the symbolic names found in the first chapter. The names by which Israel is there represented have a double interpretation—two lines of prophecy are bound up in them; the first of woe, the second of weal. Under the punitive hand of Divine justice, Gomer, *i.e.*, "completion," furnishes the idea that the measure of Israel's iniquities was full; the eldest child's name, Jezreel, "God shall scatter," foretold that the Lord would expel them from their land, and disperse them among the nations; the second child, the girl, Lo-Ruhamah, "the unpitied," foreshadows, as we have seen, the forlorn and helpless state of the nation during the time of their banishment and bondage. The history of Israel in the middle ages is the best comment on this type—a period when God seemed to have shut up His compassion, and the fiercest forms of persecution that man could devise were let loose upon them. The last child, Lo-ammi, "not my people," pictures the nation thus bereft of their inheritance, scattered to the four winds of heaven, unpitied and uncared for, now

6   I will be like the dew to Israel,
    He shall blossom like the lily;
    And shall strike his roots like (those of) Lebanon.⁷

reaching the climax of their woes—without temple, sacrifice, or priest, disowned of heaven, and branded with this name as a badge of their rejection by God, Lo-ammi. But when the Lord in the latter day visits His people—the period foretold in this chapter—then all is reversed, the second interpretation of these names comes in for fulfilment; the rule of the rod gives place to the rule of love. Gomer, " completion," conveys the hint that the mystery of God is finished. In the prayer and confession of Israel, combined with the renouncement of their idols, (verses 2, 3, we have an echo of the fact that Lo-ammi has become Ammi, " my people." In the plea for pity urged in verse 3, and answered in verse 4, we catch a glimpse of Lo-Ruhamah changed into Ruhamah, " the pitied." And in the figures borrowed from the vegetable world, of trees, and corn, and flowers, planted and nurtured by God, so that they grow in fruitfulness and fragrance, we behold Jezreel, " the scattered of God," become Jezreel, " the sown of God," possessing, and prospering in, the land which the Lord promised to Abraham and his seed for ever. It must not be omitted that the husband of Gomer and the father of the children was Hosea, *i.e.*, " Saviour." His name changes not—only one interpretation is possible here—a type of Him, who is " the same yesterday, to-day, and for ever," whose love has " no variableness," whose purposes " no shadow of turning," who, in all the long dark period of Israel's sin and suffering, has beheld the end from the beginning. Heaviness has endured its night, joy cometh in the morning. The prophecy trembles on the threshold of fulfilment—" Thy Maker is thy husband, and thy Redeemer the Holy One of Israel." (Isa. liv. 5.)

6. ⁷ " Like Lebanon." Like the roots of the cedars that

7 Spring up shall his suckers,
And like the olive-tree shall be his beauty ;
And his fragrance like (that of) Lebanon.
8 They shall be converted[8] who sit under his shade,
They shall revive (like) corn,[9]
And blossom like the vine ;
His memorial (shall be) like the wine of Lebanon.

grow on Lebanon. The reference may be to the foundations of the mountain itself, but the former interpretation seems best. The figures employed in this and the following verse suggest the following ideas: the roots, the being grounded in the faith ; the branches, the confession of faith and the producing good works ; the olive-tree, sanctification ; and the fragrance, holy influence on all around. The lily supplies an emblem for beauty, but it is fragile ; the lack of the lily is supplemented therefore by the cedar ; and the fruitless nature of the king of the forest is counteracted by the olive, the symbol of fertility. Thus each combines with the rest to give expression to the manifold graces in the treasury of Christ.

LXX., ῥίζας αὐτοῦ ὡς ὁ Λίβανος. Syr., "Radices ut Libanicas." Vulg., "Radix ejus ut Libani." Targ., "Sicut arbor Libani quæ diffundit suam propaginem."

8. [8] "They shall be converted," &c. The verb ישבו is not to be connected with the verb יחיו, as merely implying repetition, "they shall live again," but must be taken independently. This verb invariably combines the two ideas of restoration to the land, and repentance towards God. Conversion seems to be the prominent thought in the prophet's mind.

LXX., ἐπιστρέψουσι. Syr., "Reædificabuntur." Vulg., "Convertentur."

[9] "They shall revive (like) corn." The figure employed here with reference to Israel's restoration and the period of

9 (Saith) Ephraim,[10]
    What to me any more with idols ;
(*God*)     I have heard and regarded him ;
(*Ephraim*) I am like a green cypress,
(*God*)     From me thy fruit is found.

the resurrection, probably furnished the basis of our Lord's parable respecting Himself and His Church, (John xii. 24,) and also of St. Paul's illustration of the resurrection body in his essay on that mystery, (1 Cor. xv. 37.) The Targum paraphrase is so beautiful that I cannot forbear inserting it: " They shall be gathered together from the midst of their captivity; they shall dwell under the shadow of His Christ; and the dead shall live, and good shall increase on the earth."

יחיו דגן וג׳ . LXX., ζήσονται καὶ μεθυσθήσονται σίτῳ. Vulg., " Vivent tritico, et germinabunt quasi vinea." And similarly the Syr.

9. [10] Some expositors refer all this passage to God, and take " Ephraim " as a vocative case: " O Ephraim, what have I to do with idols? I have done with that controversy; you shall serve idols no more." Such interpreters find in the cypress tree, a type of the tree of life, that is, God, under whose shadow the people shall find rest. Others take " Ephraim " absolutely, and supply " shall say," יאמר ; and the following sentences then form a dialogue between the sinner and the Saviour. Ephraim confesses and renounces his sin. God says that He has heard his prayer. Ephraim, instinct with grace and new life, replies, "I am like a green cypress;" to which, with evident allusion to the fact that the cypress produces no edible or useful fruit, God answers, " From Me thy fruit is found." It is grace that works in man the fruits of the Spirit; so that good works in the believer are not his own works, but the works of God the Holy Ghost within him, and the confession of every child of God who

10  Who is wise, then shall he understand these things?
(Who is) understanding, then shall he know them?
For righteous are the ways of Jehovah,
And the just shall walk in them,
But transgressors shall fall in them.

bringeth forth much fruit, will be that of David, when he offered abundantly, "Of thine own have we given thee."

LXX., τῷ 'Εφραὶμ τί αὐτῷ ἔτι καὶ εἰδώλοις. Syr., "Quid mihi amplius cum idolis?" Vulg., "Ephraim quid mihi ultra idola?" Targ., "Quid ad nos ultra servire idolis?"

"Answered," עניתי. It will be seen that the LXX. and Syriac take the verb ענה in the sense of "humiliation," as they do in ch. ii. 17, where "answering each other" seems to be the clear interpretation of the word.

LXX., ἐταπείνωσα. So Syriac, "Humiliavi." Vulgate, "Exaudiam." Targ. supports the translation of the text.

10. "Righteous are the ways," &c. Mark the reference to Deut. xxxii. 4. The concluding chapters of Deuteronomy have a striking affinity to the closing chapter of our prophet.

Thus with a solemn charge and a personal application does our prophet close his roll, in which, though "there are many things hard to be understood," though the text may have been frequently obscure, the construction intricate, and the figures enigmatical, and as a consequence, critics and commentators at fault and variance with each other, yet the purport of the prophecy as a protest against idolatry in every shape, and as an assurance of God's love for His people, even when His hand is charged with the heaviest punishment, cannot be mistaken by the pious and prayerful student.

May the wisdom which unlocks the mysteries of the kingdom, and the grace which leads the just along the path of light and life, be vouchsafed abundantly to the reader!

LONDON:
PRINTED AT THE OPERATIVE JEWISH CONVERTS' INSTITUTION,
PALESTINE PLACE, BETHNAL GREEN, N.E.

www.ingramcontent.com/pod-product-compliance
Lightning Source LLC
Chambersburg PA
CBHW020152170426
**43199CB00010B/1000**